The Diary of
The Portsmouth, Kittery and York
Electric Railroad

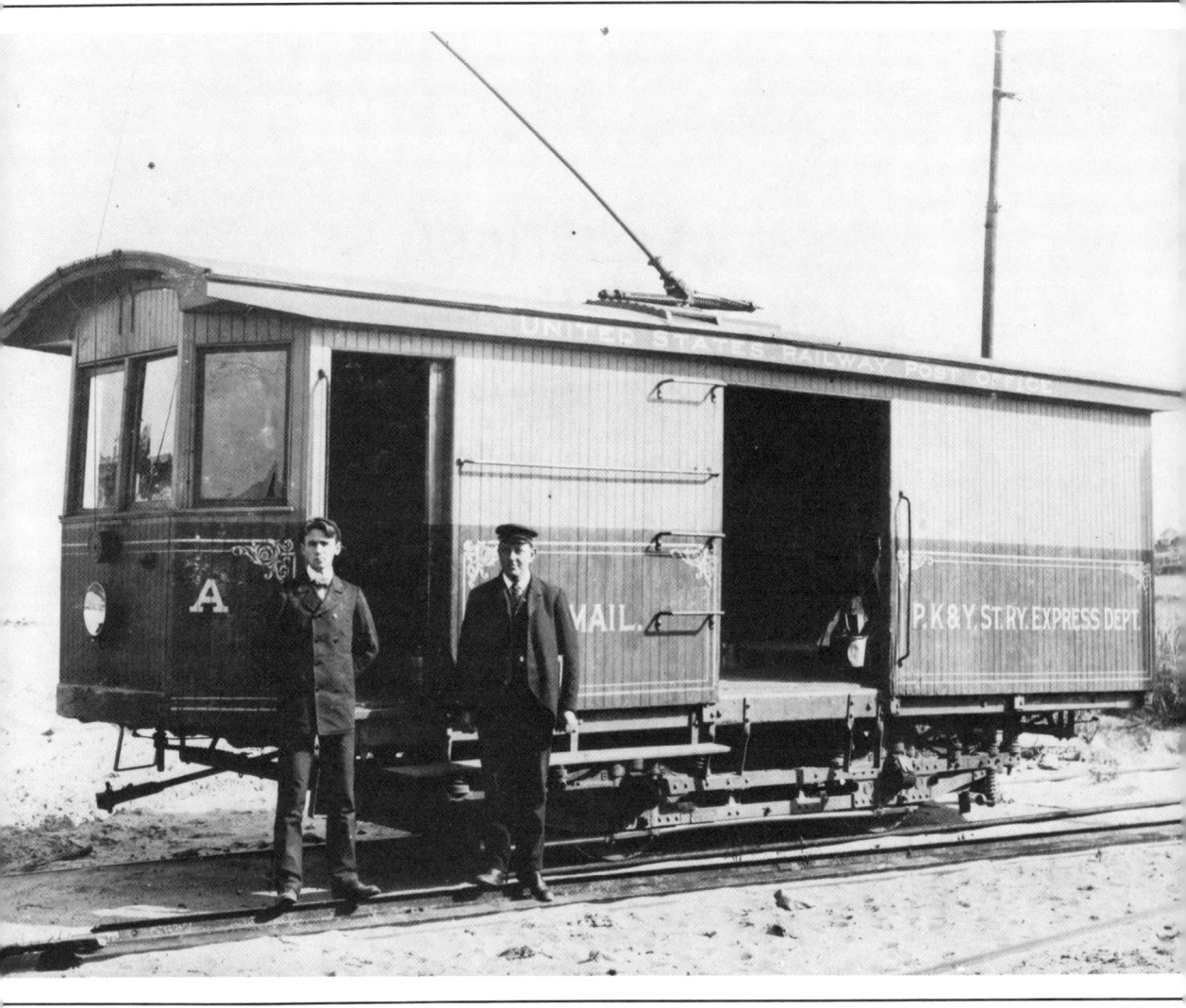

Mail Car A at York Beach. This was the original mail car which began operation in 1898. The young man on the left is Charley "Alphabetical" Davis. His companion is George Woodward. Courtesy of Howard Moulton.

We must believe that this road, though passing through your streets, will ultimately work for your glory and good.

York Courant, *April 16, 1897*

The Diary of
The Portsmouth, Kittery and York
Electric Railroad

A chronology of events based on newspaper accounts, editorials, news notes and letters to the editor from January 8, 1897 to November 12, 1897.

by
John D. Bardwell

Portsmouth Marine Society
Publication Nine

Published for the Society by
Peter E. Randall
PUBLISHER

© 1986 by John D. Bardwell
Printed in the United States of America
Designed and produced by
    Peter E. Randall Publisher
    Box 4726, Portsmouth, NH 03801

Maps by Alex Wallach.

A publication of the
    Portsmouth Marine Society
    Box 147, Portsmouth, NH 03801

Other Portsmouth Marine Society Publications:
1. John Haley Bellamy, Carver of Eagles
2. The Prescott Story
3. The Piscataqua Gundalow,
    Workhorse for a Tidal Basin Empire
4. The Checkered Career of Tobias Lear
5. Clippers of the Port of Portsmouth
    and the Men who built Them
6. Portsmouth-Built
    Submarines of the Portsmouth Naval Shipyard
7. Atlantic Heights
    A World War I Shipbuilders' Community
8. There Are No Victors Here
    A Local Perspective on the Treaty of Portsmouth

To the memory of my beloved grandmother, Elizabeth Gertrude Bardwell, who was the first to respond to my questions about travel on the "electric cars." Her wicker basket of old photographs was the source of many history lessons and her humorous stories about local characters were entertaining as well as informative. Perhaps this account of the construction of the Portsmouth, Kittery and York Electric Railroad will preserve a moment in history for those readers who did not have a grandmother to tell them about it.

Contents

Illustrations	ix
Acknowledgments	xi
Introduction	1
Construction Details and Railroad Operations	7
I Know Not What The Truth May Be, I'm Telling it to You As it was told to me.	11
A Scenic and Historic Trolley Ride	71
Epilog	79
Index	81
About the Author	84

Illustrations

Interior of a St. Louis 30′ closed car	Cover, 44
Mail car A at York Beach (Circa 1898)	ii
Car No.4 at Kittery Point in 1897	xii
Plowing snow from the tracks at the intersection of Church Street and Long Sands Road	4
Brave Boat Harbor trestle	5
Walter Frost and Archie Jewell in their uniforms	6
Mail Car 108	9
George Plaisted, Editor of the *York Courant*	10
Nevers Carriage Company building	14
View of York Corner showing Junkins' and Plaisted's stores	14
A P.K.&Y. car approaching Brave Boat Harbor trestle	16
Portsmouth, Kittery and York Street Railway, map	18
Alternative Routes, map	19
Building the trolley track through York Village	27
A view from Mercer's Corner looking toward York Harbor	28
York Harbor in 1897	30
The road lined with rails and ties near the Lancaster block	30
Miss Pickering's house in York Harbor	34
Varrell House and Annex in York Harbor	34
Hillcroft Inn before the porches were enclosed	36
York Street as it passed by Norwood Farms	36
Crossing Norton's trestle	42
Disputed trestle crossing railroad track at Seabury	42
Passengers at Bald Head Cliff station	44
Entrance to the carhouse at Kittery Point	46

An open car crossing the York River on Sewall's bridge	48
A car passing through York Village, circa 1915	48
A stage coach at the Hotel Mitchell	50
The Iduna Spring Hotel on Long Beach	50
The Kittery Point carhouse and power station, circa 1897	53
Ferry *Kittery* at Badger's Island landing	53
Ferry landing and waiting room on Badger's Island	54
Portsmouth ferry landing	54
Workmen extending the tracks to St. Aspinquid Park	58
Entrance to St. Aspinquid Park	58
The Goldenrod	60
Interior of the Goldenrod before the porch was added	60
The Lafayette Inn in York Beach	62
Double truck flatcar	65
Crossing Badger's Island trestle	70
Car at York Corner	73
Arriving at York Beach	74
Workmen removing the tracks in York Village	77
Abandoned trolley car in a York Beach field	77
Last trolley passing through Badger's Island in 1923	78

Acknowledgments

MANY PEOPLE RESPONDED to my request for information, assisted with the search for illustrations or in some way assisted with the preparation of this record. I would like to acknowledge the special help of Mrs. Charles Prince, Cynthia Hayes, Betty Winton, Phil Rowe, Harry Hutchins, Bob and Iva Moffit, Carl and Dottie Merrill, Wini Whalen, Ralph Littlefield and Doris Marston. Ted and Ray Hollingsworth have my sincere thanks for sharing their copies of the *York Courant* from which the "diary" was extracted.

O.R. Cummings and Howard Moulton provided many of the photographs. They are true experts on the history of electric street railways.

Car No. 4 at Kittery Point in 1897.

Last week, Mr. & Mrs. Samuel Blake of Kittery Point, went to York Beach on an electric car. Mrs. Blake had not visited the Beach for fifty-five years, and it was the first time she rode on a car of any kind.

York Courant, *September 10, 1897*

Introduction

THE KITTERY AND YORK ELECTRIC RAILROAD COMPANY was incorporated on March 27, 1893 to build an electric trolley line from Kittery, through Kittery Point, to York Village, York Harbor and York Beach, and to operate a ferry across the Piscataqua River between Kittery and Portsmouth, New Hampshire. On March 19, 1895, the charter was extended for two years and on February 2, 1897, another two year extension was granted.

Incorporators of the company, which was capitalized at $200,000, included Frank E. Rowell, Horace Mitchell, Calvin Hayes, Clarence M. Prince, Jethro H. Swett, Samuel E. Jennison, Charles F. McClure, John E. Norwood, Wilson L. Hawkes and Orville D. Baker. All of these men, with the exception of Mr. Baker, were residents of the Kittery-York area. Baker was an Augusta attorney, specializing in street railway matters.

Late in 1896, control of the road was acquired by Amos F. Gerald of Fairfield, one of Maine's best known street railway promoters. His associate, Isaac C. Libby of Waterville, was prominent in the Kennebec Valley lumber industry.

Leon E. Scruton of Portsmouth, a civil engineer, was engaged to lay out the route of the Kittery and York Street Railway. On February 1, 1897, at an organizational meeting, the name of the company was officially changed to the Portsmouth, Kittery and York Street Railway.

From then on, events moved rapidly. On April 10, at a special town meeting, the voters of York approved the construction of the P.K.&Y. by a 3-1 majority. On April 20, the railway's proposed route in Kittery was approved by the town fathers. Three days later, similar action was taken by the selectmen of York.

Property owners and hotel proprietors at York Harbor opposed the route through that area. They asked the State Supreme Court to enjoin the building of the railway along Norwood Farm Road (a part of the present route 1-A) and to order the company to use a route running directly from York Village to York Beach. The injunction was denied and an equity suit was dismissed.

The P.K.&Y. started its line at Badger's Island instead of at the Portsmouth Bridge. The decision not to operate over the Portsmouth Bridge was probably due to pressure from the owners of the Boston and Maine Railroad. They considered the electric railroad an unwelcome competitor for the York Harbor and Beach steam railroad which had been operating since 1877.

Construction began in the spring of 1897. The route extended from Badger's Island, Kittery, where a ferry landing and waiting station were built, over the locations named in the Kittery and York's Charter, a

> *The citizens of York Harbor are on the warpath and war has been declared against the Portsmouth and York Electric Railroad.* — York Courant, *April 30, 1897*

distance of 15.1 miles. The road, as a whole, was a very crooked one. Because it followed the shore, some 13 pile trestles, totaling nearly 1.3 miles in length, were required to cross the numerous creeks, coves and harbors along the route.

In mid-April, George E. Macomber of Augusta was engaged to handle the grading and track laying. Other contracts were awarded for the construction of trestles and bridges, the building and equipping of the Kittery Point carhouse and power station and the furnishing of the rolling stock.

More than 60 laborers were hired by the contractor and construction began early in May. The target date for completion was July 1st, but this was delayed by the injunction proceedings instituted by the York Harbor group. However, the charter required that the electric railway be in business no later than September 1, 1897.

A ferry slip and waiting station were built by the P.K.&Y. at the foot of Market Street in Portsmouth. A wooden frame carhouse and brick power station were built at Kittery Point, with another carhouse at York Beach. Rolling stock, consisting of four single truck closed cars, two 10-bench four-wheel open cars and seven 14-bench four-wheel open cars and seven 14-bench double truck opens, was purchased from the Briggs Carriage Company. Other equipment included a single truck mail car and a snow plow. There were two ferryboats, the "New March," formerly the "Brownstone" and the "Mystic." The "New March" burned to the water's edge in 1899 and was replaced by a new ferry, "The Kittery." In 1901, they disposed of the "Mystic" and acquired a small steamer named the "Alice Howard."

The ferry service was intended to be temporary for it was the plan of the P.K.&Y. to promote the building of a bridge across the river between Badger's Island and a point near St. John's Church in Portsmouth. This plan did not materialize and the lack of direct access to Portsmouth was to plague the company and its successors for many years.

A 600-foot bridge, 24-feet wide, for trolleys and teams, connected Badger's Island with the mainland. At Seabury and York Harbor, overhead bridges were built to span the York Harbor and Beach Railroad. It was necessary for the P.K.&Y. to strengthen the Kittery Point highway bridge and Sewall's bridge at York to make them safe for the weight of the electric car.

Operations began on August 12, 1897, when the first car traversed the entire line. Only limited service was available until the 27th of that month, with two cars running over the four miles of line between Badger's Island and the Kittery Point carhouse. Regular service to York Village commenced on October 6th and to York Harbor and York Beach on June 30th of the following year.

The Portsmouth, Kittery and York was one of the first street railways in New England to operate a post office car. It was given a

> *It is admitted that the York Harbor people do not want the road to go through the Harbor.*
> York Courant, *April 2, 1897*

four-year contract in 1897 to carry the mail between Portsmouth and York Beach.

Two double truck closed cars, one built by Wason and the other by St. Louis Car Company, were acquired in 1899 and 1900, respectively. To improve the power at York Beach, a sizable storage battery bank was installed there.[1]

Late in 1899, the railway purchased St. Aspinquid Park, a pleasure resort at the north end of York Beach, near the Cape Neddick River. Created a year earlier by Henry E. Evans, this park contained a large

Clearing the snow at the corner of Church Street and Long Sands Road.

octagonal dance hall, a cafe which offered fish dinners and a menagerie which included a large bear. It was attractively landscaped with walks, carriage drives and rustic arbors. The P.K.&Y. built a .4 mile extension from the original terminus at York Beach Square to the resort entrance in the spring of 1900.

The total cost of the Portsmouth, Kittery and York Street Railway as of June 30, 1903 was $511,837, covered in part by $221,700 in common capital stock (2,217 shares at $100 par) and $200,000 in 6 percent 20 year gold bonds, issued as of March 1, 1897 and maturing on March 1, 1917. The Waterville Trust Company of Waterville, Maine, which had provided most of the construction funds, was trustee of the first mortgage securing the bonds. There were 108 stockholders, 28 of whom were Maine residents, with a total of 706 shares.

Commenting on the construction of the P.K.&Y., the Railroad Commissioner's report for 1897 said in part:

> This is the longest electric railroad constructed in Maine during the year. Beginning at York Beach in the town of York, it extends through the towns of York and Kittery to Badger's Island in said

PORTSMOUTH, KITTERY AND YORK ELECTRIC RAILROAD

Brave Boat Harbor trestle was one of the thirteen pile trestles between Kittery and York. Nearly 1.3 miles of trestles were required to cross the creeks, coves and harbors along the route.

Kittery, thence connecting with the City of Portsmouth, N.H., by a steam ferry.

Following as it does the seacoast, there are many pile and trestle bridges, these being 13 in number with a total length of nearly 1.3 miles. These are largely built of hemlock, with a fair margin of safety, and while safe for the present, will need careful watching.[2]

---

[1] Cummings, Osmond R. "A History of the Atlantic Shoreline Railway," *Transportation*, the Connecticut Electric Railway Association, Vol. 4-150, pp. 12-14.
[2] Cummings, O.R., *Trolleys to York Beach*, Privately Printed, 1964.

Walter Frost, seated, and Archie Jewell were photographed in their uniforms. Courtesy of Ralph Littlefield.

Construction Details

ROADBED CONSTRUCTION on the York Beach line represented the company's latest and best practice. The greater part of the line was ballasted with gravel, but rock was also used where available. The rails were of 80-lb. T-Section, laid in thirty-three foot lengths. The rails were on six inch square ties, eight feet long, spaced two feet apart. The ties on tangents were usually of chestnut, but oak was used on some of the curves.

The poles on the York Beach line were of cedar or chestnut. Those carrying high-tension lines were thirty-five feet long, but other poles were three to five feet shorter. Owing to the frequent heavy winds, it was considered advisable to anchor all poles. The guy wires had wooden insulators to minimize current leakage. Two cross-arms were provided for two three-phase 10,000-volt transmission circuits. The trolley wire was suspended from brackets to give a clearance of eighteen feet above the head of the rails.

The steam plant at Kittery Point provided the power supply. This was a direct-current station containing two Ball & Wood engines, belted to 225-kw and 110-kw General Electric generators and one Erie City engine running a second 225-kw generator. There was also a battery of 220 cells at York Beach, and a 300 kw Westinghouse rotary and transformer located at York Corner.

All dispatching was done by telephone to the carhouses, substations and booths placed at the turnouts. Pegged boards were used by the dispatchers to follow the progress of cars in their charge. All stations and turnouts were named for the convenience of dispatching. The scheme was also of value to the passengers, inasmuch as every turnout was furnished with a locality sign.

The dispatcher's orders were usually received by the carhouse or substation attendants, who wrote them out on autographic registers. They delivered one copy to the motorman and another to the conductor, while the third copy remained in the locked box. In cases when a car was delayed for over five minutes, the motorman had to call up the dispatcher at the first turn-out, receive his order and repeat it to the conductor. The conductor repeated the message to the dispatcher before proceeding. In busy times it was customary for the station men at York Beach, and other important points, to keep the dispatcher informed of the progress of the cars.

During periods of heavy traffic, the company ran cars two or more in a block, in the car-following system. The first car carried a sign worded "Car Following," instead of having the customary green sign. This served as an indication to waiting passengers that there was a car behind. Upon reaching a turn-out the crew of this car notified the opposing car to wait for No. 2. Should No. 2 bear a "Car Following" sign, it was necessary to wait for No. 3, and so on. "Following cars" were not subject to dispatcher's orders. Their operators were instructed to obey the orders given to the preceeding car.

In general, fares were based on a rate of two cents a mile. The fifteen-and-a-half mile trip between York Beach and Portsmouth cost

The freightyard at the depot has been the center of attraction for large numbers since last Friday, when two of the electric cars arrived. They are of the open pattern, ten seats, and like the ordinary cars run in the large cities.   York Courant, *July 9, 1897*

twenty-five cents. During the first year of operation, the electric line earned $75,000 on the twenty-five cent fare for an hour-and-a-half trip. It took over the mail, and beat the steam railroad on rates for local express. Local pleasure riding was induced by giving free concerts at certain parks along the line. The fare zones were allowed to overlap to include churches, post offices or other points. School tickets, good only on school days, were sold at reduced rates. Certain workmen also qualified for reduced rate tickets. Tickets could be purchased in special buildings or in village stores, where waiting rooms were provided.

During the summer months, the coastal lines were operated on a

Mail car 108 at York Beach. Courtesy of Howard Moulton.

half-hour schedule. If traffic was heavy, two or three cars were run in a block on the "Car Following" system. Otherwise, cars were run every hour. Winter schedules called for fewer cars because of a reduction in the number of passengers.

The company carried mail in a combination mail and express car, receiving ¾ cent per mile for each lineal foot of car. Thus, a twelve foot car returned eight cents per mile traveled. Closed pouch mail was carried at three cents a mile.[3]

---

[3] Information from *Street Railway Journal*, Vol. XXX, No. 24, December 14, 1907.

George Plaisted, Editor of the York Courant.

I Know Not What the Truth May Be, I'm Telling it to You As it was told to me.

George Plaisted, Editor
The *York Courant*

THE FOLLOWING NEWS ARTICLES were published in the weekly *York Courant* during the period when the electric railroad was organized and constructed. Several points of view are presented which illustrate the impact of this new technology on the people of this small, rural community.

January 8, 1897

It May Be A Go

It looks as if the parties who have visited Portsmouth off and on for the past two weeks looking up electric railroad interests mean business. On Saturday they visited F. H. Hardman, the bicycle dealer and arranged with him to send a man over the York Beach route to get the distance with a cyclometer attached to the wheel. One of Mr. Hardman's men left the Kittery end of the Portsmouth bridge, passing through Kittery and Kittery Point to Brave Boat Harbor, across to Harris Cove and thence to York Beach via the lower road. The distance from Portsmouth bridge to Union Bluff over the proposed route was exactly twelve and five-eights miles.

Horace Mitchell of Kittery Point is interested in the proposed electric road. He visited Badger's Island and made the owners of the island good offers for their property. The projectors of the new enterprise propose to establish an electric ferry across to Kittery passing over Badger's Island. On the island they plan to erect a big hotel which will command a view of the river, and harbor.

January 15, 1897

Latest in Electrics

Twenty-five Mile Road to Be Equipped in York County

It was reported in the *Biddeford Journal* that Messrs. A.F. Gerald of Fairfield and I.C. Libby of Waterville, well known Maine electric railroad men, have just completed arrangements to become owners of the Portsmouth, Kittery and York Beach Railroad. The line will be twenty-five miles long and will extend along York Beach to York Village, past the Navy Yard to Portsmouth, admirably accomodating a large territory. This is one of the most important railroad deals ever made in Maine. The promoters plan to have the road in operation by July 18, 1897.

The Legislature of Maine granted a charter for the road in 1893. By the terms of the charter, their right to build would be forfeited unless $20,000 should be expended on the road by next March. The sum will immediately be spent on the road.

The line will include a steam ferry across the Piscataqua River between Kittery and Portsmouth, connecting the two states with a craft large enough to take on teams and cars. This ferry is scheduled to be in operation by May 1st.

The road will be one of the most modern electric railroads in the country, "commencing" as Mr. Libby graphically expresses it, "where other New England roads left off."

All the cars and equipment are to be of the most improved type. The fares will be low and the service prompt. Transportation in this vicinity will be revolutionized.

January 22, 1897

No Electric Railroad

Hon. Henry E. Evans, in reply to a question as to how the electric railroad was progressing in York, stated that as yet there were no signs that anything is happening.

"In my mind," said Mr. Evans, "Nothing of the kind will be done this year. The people of York do not want it. Another thing, if an electric railroad should be put in there and it should cut into the summer receipts of the York Harbor and Beach railroad, we have the privilege of stopping the service during the winter months.

"As it is now, the winter service is continued at considerable loss to the company. If the summer receipts are reduced, it may become impracticable to continue running winters.

"The scheme seems to be a move to get a continuance of the charter. If the ten percent of the stock, or $20,000 were to be expended before the time called for, something more definite would have been done before now."

Change of Name

A petition has been presented to the Maine Legislature to change the name of the Kittery and York electric railroad to Portsmouth and York street railway.

A Sure Thing

A Director of the Electric Railroad Says Road Will Be Built

There is some doubt in the minds of many citizens as to whether the proposed electric railroad from Portsmouth to York Beach is simply talk or if the backers of the scheme mean business. A representative of the press called upon one of the directors and asked, "Do you intend to build a road from Portsmouth to York Beach within the next year?"

He answered, "I wish I was as sure of living a hundred years as I am that the road will be constructed before this time next year." Said he, "There is not a particle of truth in the stories regarding the sale of the road. The Boston and Maine R.R. would benefit by the line in many ways."

It is known that the new owners are in Boston making business arrangements. The parties interested in the Kittery project expect building to begin this month.

January 29, 1897

Editorial

That the electric railroad through York is to be built, sooner or later, there is hardly a doubt. Whether it will be a benefit to York as a whole, is a question that no man can answer with any degree of certainty; and whether it will pay or not, is a matter of much doubt.

Nevers Carriage Company, located opposite the library in York Village. The building also housed Lyman Littlefield's blacksmith shop, the Bone & Young auto repair shop and Raymond Earl's sign shop. Courtesy of Leon Ramsdell.

View of York Corner showing Junkin's store on the left and Plaisted's store on the right. Courtesy of Peter Moore.

The York Harbor and Beach Railroad has been of inestimable value to York. The only error its planners made, was in running such a circuitous, crooked and expensive route. Nature had almost built a roadbed in a straight line, which would have reduced the expense of building as well as the running expenses for as long as the road exists.

The expenses of the road have to be met and the passenger tariff is high, as compared with other railroads. However, we must remember that the road is run through the winter months at a loss. It is actually a summer road and its receipts are like those of a summer hotel. They are necessarily higher than an-all-the-year-round, and yet much cheaper than the lumbering old stage coach of a dozen years ago.

The railroad, by its charter, has the power to suspend business through the winter months, and it is hinted that this will happen if the Electric Trolley Company reduces its summer receipts. It would probably please the electric people if the railroad ceased operations in the winter. We understand that the trolley cars will be prepared to carry freight as well as passengers. This would give them all of the business between Portsmouth and York.

The electric road, with its low fares, could seriously damage the steam road because the passengers naturally would ride at the least expense.

We do not anticipate the building of the electric road this season, for we have learned on good authority that the selectmen of Kittery will oppose the running of the line on much of the highway. The matter will be referred to the county commissioners and from them an appeal may be taken to the Supreme Court. This will take time, hence our belief that it will not be built right away.

We are aware that the project has pretty solid backing, and we must disagree with our friend Evans about its being a bluff. The road will be built and York Corner will be left out in the cold as it was with the steam road. But we believe that an electric road will eventually be built from So. Berwick to York, so that riding accommodations will be plenty and good. We await the result with no great anxiety.

(George F. Plaisted)

A P.K.&Y. Briggs 14' bench car approaching the Brave Boat Harbor trestle.

February 5, 1897

Stockholders of the Portsmouth Electric Road Elect Officers
Messrs., Gerald and Libbey Both Say That The Road Is A Go

The stockholders of the Portsmouth, Kittery and York Electric Railroad held a meeting Monday afternoon at 3 o'clock in the offices of Judge Samuel W. Emery, Franklin Block, Portsmouth and elected officers as follows:

Directors: H.F. Gerald, Fairfield, Me.; I.C. Libbey, Waterville; Chas. Milliken, Augusta; Horace Mitchell, Kittery Point and Lewis E. Staples, Portsmouth.

Pres., A.F. Gerald; Treas., I.C. Libbey; Clerk, Samuel W. Emery.

Messrs. Gerald and Libbey are indignant over the reports in circulation that the road is not to be built and say that it is a sure go.

February 12, 1897

May Erect a Big Hotel

An agent for a syndicate of wealthy Lowell gentlemen was in town Saturday to inspect a site near where the old Bartlett house stood. If the electric railroad is a success, these gentlemen contemplate erecting a large summer hotel modeled somewhat after the style of the Wentworth.

February 19, 1897

Laid out the York Route

A.F. Gerald and Senator Horace Mitchell were in York Monday to go over the route of the electric road through this town. The selectmen are much in favor of the line there. Senator Mitchell said the rails will arrive here before March 1st and work will start at once.

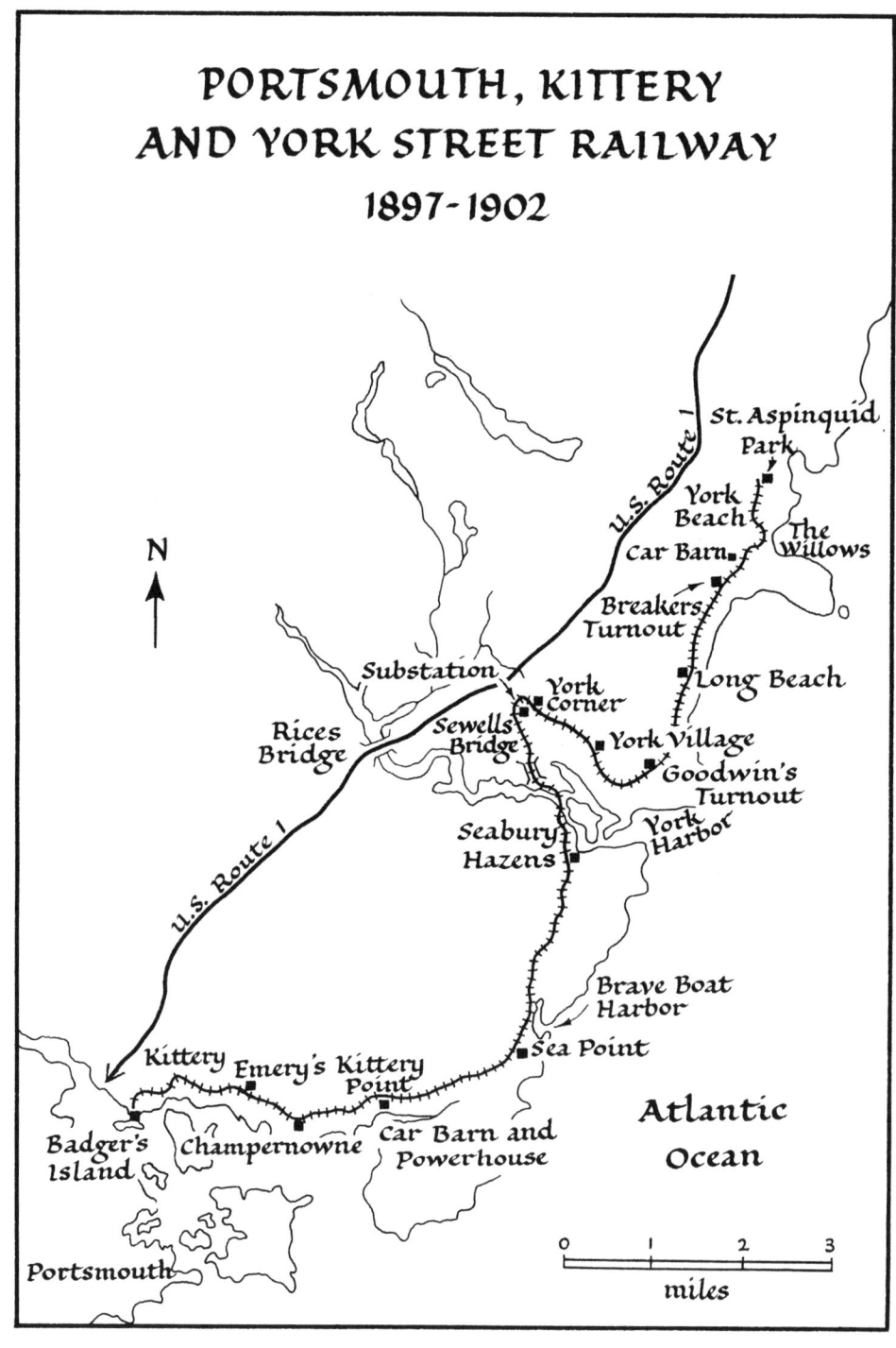

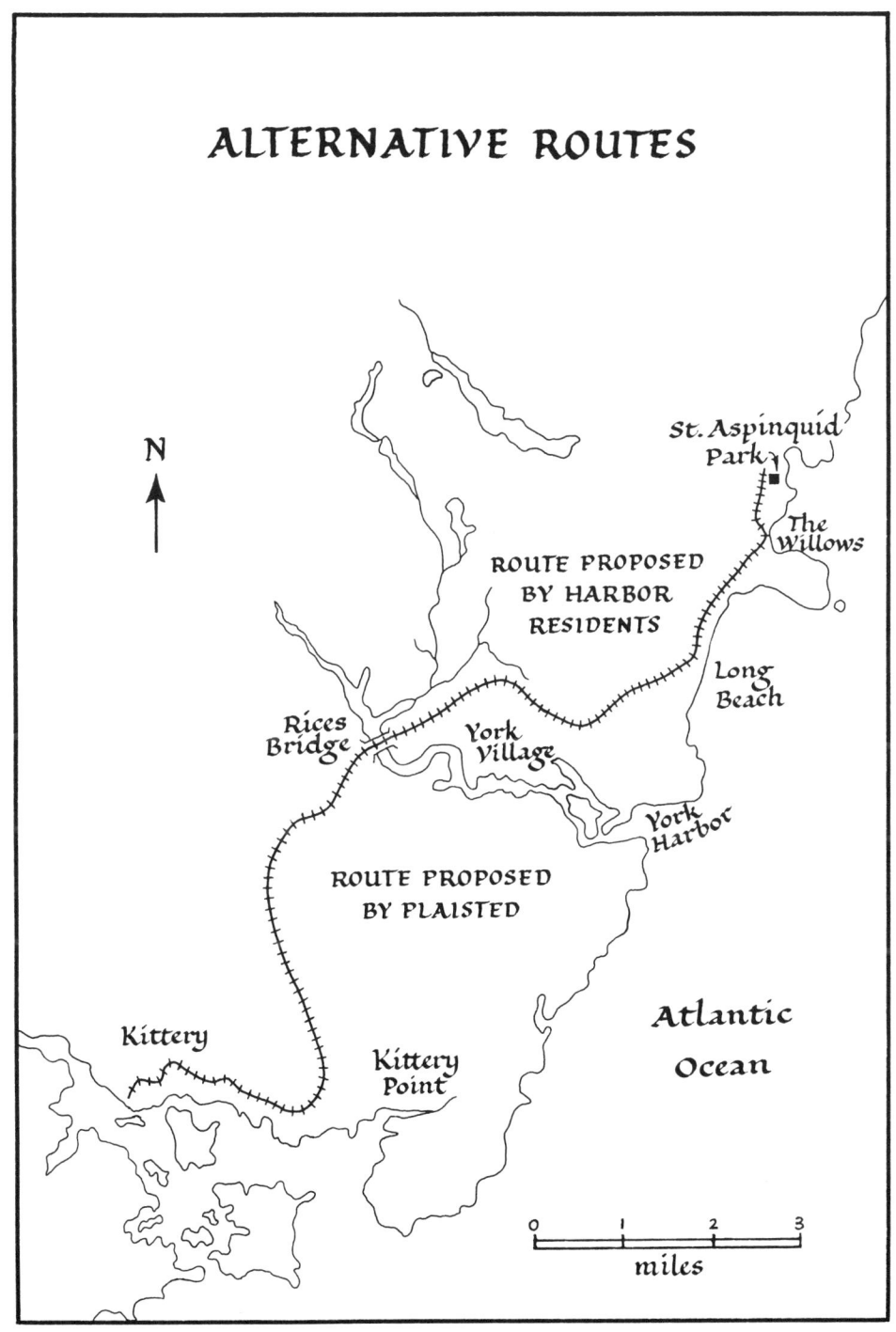

February 26, 1897

It seems the electric people, in their survey, are following the wake of the railroad people who now bitterly rue the day they planted their road where they did.

The electric people are keeping east of the Y.H.&B., all the way. The route passes through swamps and marshes from Kittery Point to York Harbor, necessitating the building of over a mile of piling at a cost of $12 per foot, or over $60,000 for piling alone—besides other bridges.

Now if they would start from their ferry landing at Kittery Foreside, running to Kittery Point, cross the Y.H.&B. by an overhead bridge at the deep cut near the hotel, then come to the post road via the J.T. Lewis road — follow the post road to and over Rice's Bridge to York Corner and York Village, over the Y.H.&B. overhead bridge to York Harbor, thence to York Beach by the shore, they would thus avoid the enormous expense of so much pile bridging and other bridges required by the proposed route over marshes and swamps.

There would certainly be more patronage on this route than on the other. After leaving Kittery Point proper there is nothing on the proposed route until York Harbor is reached. On this line there are fifty houses from Rice's Bridge to York Village, in addition to the houses on the side roads. The Harbor business would be obtained just the same, in addition to business on Long Beach and York Beach proper.

The distance is not greater over the route we propose, and it would save nearly $100,000 on the construction of bridges, besides the additional expense of bridge repairs.

This certainly seems to us the most feasible route that can be found. It is the least expensive to build and to keep in repair, and the best paying.

We hope the Electic people will not make the same mistake which the Y.H.&B. did which they now see in sorrow and regret.

The Electric Railroad

Stockholders Meet Today and Increase the Capital Stock

The stockholders of the Portsmouth and York Electric Railroad Company held a meeting in Kittery this afternoon, and voted to increase the capital stock of the company from $50,000 to $200,000. The matter of changing the route from the proposed bridge was discussed, and it was the opinion that the line should cross Sewall's Bridge. The sleepers and poles have been ordered, and will be placed along the route within the next two weeks. The rails should arrive in Portsmouth this week.

April 2, 1897

The talk that if the electric road is not allowed to come over Sewall's Bridge, they will not come through York at all, is all moonshine and a cheap moon at that. The time is not far away when a road from Boston to Portland via York Corner will be a fact, and if these fellows want to be "in it" now is the time.

In another column we have printed the petition of a number of the most influential citizens of York asking for a special town meeting which will doubtless be held Saturday, April 10, at 2 o'clock, p.m. A

> *The citizens of the town are practically unanimous that the most practical route for the electric railroad is over the Post Road and Rice's Bridge by way of York Corner....*
> York Courant, *April 2, 1897*

petition is also in circulation, with many signers, requesting the Selectmen to use all honorable means to induce the Electric Railroad Company to locate its lines over and upon Rice's Bridge, and thence through York Corner to York Village.

There are powerful reasons why this line should be located this way. These reasons can be discussed under a single proposition. *The citizens of the town are practically unanimous that the most practical route for the electric road is over the Post Road and Rice's Bridge by way of York Corner, thence to York Village and to York Beach.*

It may be stated here that the citizens of Kittery want the road located from Badger's Island to Kittery Point, thence over Spruce Creek and Brave Boat Harbor to Seabury. It is also understood that this is the route which the projectors of the road intend to build if they can get the necessary permit from the Selectmen of York. Now this is a very nice scheme from the standpoint of the interests of our Kittery neighbors, but where are the interests of York?

In common parlance or to use a little slang, York "ain't in it." How many people are there in York who can get any good from an electric road running from Seabury station through Rayne's Neck and Brave

Boat Harbor to Kittery Point? What the people want is an electric road which will do the greatest good to the greatest number and any man who is endowed with common sense, knows that the route is over the Post Road. The idea of running an electric road through the tide water flats and unoccupied territory of the town of York, just because that is what the Kittery people want, is a plan of action which most citizens of York will earnestly oppose. The Selectmen of York will do well to consider whether they are going to grant the electric people rights over the town's roads and bridges because it suits Kittery interests or if York interests should be considered.

There is another serious question under consideration; that is whether, after reaching York Village, the line of the road shall go to York Beach by way of York Harbor or leave out the Harbor. *It is admitted that the Harbor people do not want the road to go through the Harbor.* If they do not, and there can be found feasible routes from the Village to York Beach, we see no reason why the road should be forced upon the Harbor people. They are unquestionably honest and sincere in their opinions that the road will injure Harbor interests. Whether their opinion is a mistake or not, the York Harbor people know that their fellow townsmen are too honest and considerate to foster any scheme upon them which will injure the property interests of York Harbor.

Let the town meeting be held. Let the people be heard, so that their servants in high places will know how best to protect York's interest in the way of getting the electric road where it will do some good, both to the people and the projectors.

April 9, 1897

The town of York, through its Selectmen, has the right to decide upon which of the two bridges across the York River they will permit the Portsmouth, Kittery and York Street Railway to locate its track. They can, by doing so, dictate whether the Electric Road shall be constructed over the Post Road through York Corner to the Village or whether this road shall be built purely in the interest of Kittery alone. Having it come through Kittery Point, Spruce Creek, Brave Boat Harbor and Seabury, gives the Kittery Point people a direct line of communication between the Kittery Point boarding houses and the prosperous hotels of York Beach, Long Beach and York Harbor. As a result, the half filled boarding house of lean Kittery Point may top the thriving business of the popular and well filled summer hotels of fat York. The Kittery Point hotel

landlords think they are playing a shrewd game and they think the people of York are too stupid to see through their game; but they are mistaken. York is head and shoulders ahead of Kittery Point in growth and prosperity as a summer resort. Any Selectman of York who is afraid to block this Kittery Point scheme is a traitor to York's interest and to the public sentiment of York. In fairness to the Selectmen of York, it may be said that they will gladly welcome an expression from the town as to what they should do in the way of granting locations which will make the Electric Road of value to York's interest as well as the interest of Kittery Point. If any of the Selectmen are in doubt as to their having control over the two bridges over the York River, they have only to read the Charter of the Portsmouth, Kittery and York Street Railway. The charter itself determines the rights of the town.
Here it is:

Sec. 6. "Said Company shall be authorized to lay its tracks along and over any bridge in either of said towns of Kittery and York, now constructed or that shall hereafter be constructed by either of said towns across tide waters WITH THE CONSENT OF THE MUNICIPAL OFFICERS FIRST OBTAINED and operate its cars over same."

The above is the section of law. Any man of common intelligence who needs the opinion of a lawyer to tell him the meaning of such plain English is a fool, and what fool lawyer will say the above section does not give the selectmen the right to determine which bridge, the electric road shall use.

The Selectmen under Section 3 of the charter of this electric railway have also the right to say to the electric people — "WE WILL NOT APPROVE OF YOUR CONSTRUCTING YOUR LINE FROM YORK VILLAGE TO YORK HARBOR."

Read this section for yourself. Here it is;

Section 3. This company shall have the right from the going into force or double track railway, with the necessary side track, switches and turnouts, and other appliances for operating its cars upon and along such streets, roads or highways within the towns of Kittery and York, in the county of York, as they may deem practicable, SUBJECT TO THE APPROVAL OF THE MUNICIPAL OFFICERS OF EITHER OF SAID TOWNS.:

York voters, you should think twice before you allow your Selectmen to make a mistake which cannot be undone for all time to come. If you build your schoolhouses in the wrong place you can tear them down and build others but you cannot tear up the street railway track after it is down. So, tell your Selectmen where you want it. Tell them you will not allow them to shirk their responsibility under the pretext that the law compels them to let the Electric Road go over any bridge or town road where schemers say it shall go. There is no such law. The projectors of the road can not force the town (through the Commissioners) to go where they please. You have read the law with your own eyes.

April 16, 1897

Electrical

The air is full of it! The town meeting which was well advertised in the COURANT was held on Saturday, with Hon. John C. Stewart as moderator. It was a full meeting, and some of the people were the same way. Among the out-of-town men were Messrs. A.F. Gerald, S.H. Nye, and E.J. Lawrence of Fairfield, I.C. Libbey of Waterville, William Fish of Boston, Hon. Horace Mitchell of Kittery, projectors, officers and

> *It was amusing to see persons from the back part of town, some of whom never saw an electric car, voting to force the road on to the Harbor people.*
>
> York Courant, *April 16, 1897*

stockholders of the Portsmouth, Kittery & York Beach Electric Railroad Company — together with their attorney, Hon. Herbert M. Heath of Augusta, and Hon. John W. Emery, Mayor of Portsmouth.

Unanimous consent was given Hon. H.M. Heath to address the meeting, which he did in his usual candid and argumentative manner. Then, A.F. Gerald Esq. addressed the meeting. He is a very candid man, whose good nature was conspicuous on his round face. Like Santa Clause "he shakes when he laughs like a bowl full of jelly."

J.T. Davidson presented a resolution instructing the selectmen to locate over Rices Bridge and none other, thence to the Village and York Beach leaving out the Main Street to the Harbor. This movement was wrong in its inception, and was promptly killed by an overwhelming majority.

Finally the selectmen were instructed to do just whatever the electric people wanted them to do, and if the electric people want to lay their tracks under the York River the Selectmen must say: "Oh, yes,

Messrs." But on the other hand, according to the opinion by Mr. Heath—and he is one of the ablest lawyers of Maine—the Selectmen are under no obligations to take any notice of the towns instructions. They are, he says, simply the agents of the state and do not act in their capacity as Selectmen.

We learn that the harbor people are very upset over the result of the meeting. Now brethren, the only way to be manly is to accept the inevitable in a manly spirit. The road is coming (sometime). We must take it as it is and as it comes, and while we "cornerites" are not so well pleased as we might have been had the route been differently arranged, we console with you in your "sad afflictions." We must believe that this road, though passing through your streets, will ultimately work for your glory and good. We are pained to learn that some of the people in the upper part of town who (unwisely) voted against keeping the electrics out of the Harbor are to be boycotted in selling their produce. Such methods do not help anybody. The radical remarks being heaped upon some of the corner people are as unwise as they are unjust. Brethren, let us dwell in harmony.

They Stand By Their Friends

In sending us a nice order for printing for his hotel, one of the Harbor hotel proprietors casually remarks: "When the electric railroad gets in, we propose to set this place off from the Village and establish churches, banks, etc., for ourselves and do all our trading in Portsmouth. We will sue the town for all damages of property at the Harbor. Give them h--- in your paper."

The COURANT has been strongly in favor of the Post Road route, but never has believed that the electrics should be forced upon the Harbor people or their Main Street, if they did not want it. They are honest in the belief that it will be an injury to them. There is no question that the Harbor will survive and continue to be populated with a good class of people. If one goes away because of the electrics another will take his place, and so on. Let us hope for the best.

That Town Meeting

It was amusing to see persons from the back part of town, some of whom never saw an electric car, voting to force the road onto the Harbor people.

Men whose bread and butter comes largely from the Harbor did the same thing. True they had a right to—but many things men have a right to do don't look well nor is it good economy.

Any citizen of York who goes into Kittery now, is chafed by remarks such as, "Well, we own your town." "Well, we carried everything our own way at your town meeting," etc., etc.

Just to accommodate a few families on Gerrish Island and Kittery Point the road is carried where it ought not to go, and away from where it should go, and these projectors will find out the truth of these remarks at a later period—same as the Y.H.&B. have learned about their road.

April 23, 1897

York Beach

If York Beach is to be so severely censured for wishing to "share the luxuries" of our electric railroad with our neighbors at the Harbor, they have the satisfaction of being willing to divide the good, or evil, that may come from that source. If evil, "Misery likes company," if good, "Generosity thy name is York Beach."

Gold seems to be the standard of greatness in one part of our town, and it does not seem necessary to be the possessor of it, but in order to stand head and shoulders above our neighbors, you simply have to cater to, or be the servants of those who do possess it.

News and Notes

Work on the Portsmouth, Kittery and York electric railroad began Tuesday at Kittery.

The Harbor people are kicking of too much railroad—the Village and Corner people are kicking because of too little water, and so we are drifting—all in a "happy frame of mind."

Two carloads of electric railroad ties arrived at York Beach, Tuesday.

Work on the electric road is being rushed. Another lot of Italians arrived last Friday, which, in addition to those already here, make a large gang.

York Courant, *June 11, 1897*

One of the crew who built the electric trolley track through York Village. Ralph Tabor photograph.

April 30, 1897

War at York Harbor

Hotel Men Doing All In Their Power To Defeat The Electric Road

The citizens of York Harbor are on the warpath and war has been declared against the Portsmouth and York Electric Railroad. The citizens of that section are in a turmoil over the fact that the road is to pass through that part of the town. It is asserted by the leading men there that the road will not be built through the Harbor and everything possible is being done to succeed in carrying out their threats.

At the town meeting the board of selectmen were instructed to

A view from Mercer's Corner looking toward York Harbor. The Pickering house on the right was torn down and the area became Gilman Moulton Park. Ralph Tabor photograph.

assist the promoters of the road in every way possible and now some of the property owners at York Harbor are asking the selectmen to refuse the road the right to pass through the Harbor. The fight is a bitter one and the men who are fighting the road at the Harbor are to do everything in their power to defeat the company. The general opinion is that the road will win in the end but the men opposing it will be able to delay its construction for some time.

The Harbor people are justifiably bitter in their opposition to this decision and will fight it to the bitter end, over two thousand dollars having already been subscribed for the purpose. The best legal talent in Maine will be secured, the constitutionality of the charter will be tested, and the electric people can safely rest on their oars for a while at least. The battle will be fought inch by inch.

News and Notes

The electric roads have had their hubs driven through the "disputed corner" (York Harbor) as they call it.

The first car load of rails for the electric road arrived at Kittery Point, Monday. They are sixty feet long and weigh about 1200 pounds each. G. Frank Austin has the contract for delivering them along the line.

Bill in Equity

Portsmouth and York Electric Railway, Other Suits and Notices

A bill in equity for $50,000 has been brought against the electric road, and it was served on the clerk of the road, Wednesday evening.

Notices had previously been served on the Clerk that damages would be claimed, and of the informality of their method of procedure. Notice has also been served upon the selectmen of York, that they, too, would be held responsible for failing to proceed legally in the matter. Hot Times! Mr. Gerald says that nothing but his incarceration in Alfred jail will prevent the building of the road through the Harbor streets.

Kittery Point

A gang of Italians arrived here Saturday night to work on the electric road. Material for the power station and car house has arrived. The work of cutting down the hill at the western end of Kittery Point bridge was commenced on Monday. It will be built immediately, on the lot purchased for the purpose.

Some of our rich summer visitors, it is said, are very much opposed to the electric road, and say they will sell out if the road is put in operation. Let them sell, "there are others" that will pay the taxes.

May 7, 1897

News and Notes

A carload of one hundred Italians arrived at Kittery, Monday, to work on the electric road.

Five carloads of ties and six car loads of rails for the electric road have arrived at the York Harbor station. The rails are being distributed from York Village to York Harbor (the disputed corner) so called, by G. Frank Austin and Hayes Moulton.

York Harbor in 1897. The two houses on the left were moved together to form the Emerson Hotel. Ralph Tabor photograph.

The road is lined with rails and ties for the electric trolley. The Lancaster building is in the background. Ralph Tabor photograph.

May 14, 1897

Electrics

The state of feeling existing in our quiet town is greatly to be deplored. Citizens, who have always maintained friendly relations toward each other, now seem almost ready to fight, and why is this? Mainly because of a difference of opinion about the coming electric road. I fail to see why a person who believes in its desirability should not express that opinion, and advocate it, without awakening such a bitter spirit in those who oppose it. We should at least allow others the same rights as we claim for ourselves.

Now the class of people that will take advantage of this way of travel, will not be any more anxious to stop at the beautiful private residences at the Harbor, or trespass upon their grounds, than the owners will be to have them. They have no more affinity for the fine people at the Harbor, than the latter have for them. And we are not near a large city. That might be an objection to this way of travel, bringing the scum of a large city, out to the beaches, so there is no danger of York becoming a "Coney Island."

It has been suggested that the "power behind the throne" that has instigated and encouraged this bitter feeling, is the Boston & Maine Railroad and the truth of the adage that "corporations have no souls" is well illustrated in the course advised by these agents. Our friends at the Harbor are only injuring their own property by decrying it as they have been doing. Probably, not one would sell their houses or lands for a mill less than they have here-to-fore valued them, and we do not think that the success of the electric road will depreciate property at the Harbor in the remotest degree. We feel sure that, when this excitement is over, and the citizens at the Harbor exercise their good common sense once more, they will recognize the fact that the rest of the townspeople have rights. The good of the majority should not be sacrificed to a small minority. I am sure no one has any desire to see the Harbor injured or less prosperous than it has been. Electric railroads are in the line of progress and we should not "stay its wheels," but give to all.   FAIR PLAY

Advantage of a Trolley System

Some residents of York are taking action to prevent the destruction of her highways and the spoilation of her road beds by an electric street railway. This shows the sagacity and public spirit of some of her citizens. They deserve the support of the whole town, but will have to be content with the sympathy and companionship of the far-sighted ones who are in the minority.

There is some question of the picturesqueness of a trolley line. How will it beautify the streets as well as add to the comfort of the lovers of carriage riding? The beauty of its square, painted poles that line the streets with tiresome regularity; all provided with their square iron

> *To the laboring man with his little family who wishes for an outing of a day, it says: "Keep Out, this is no place for you, we don't want you with your lunch basket; only those who are able to pay $1.50 for a dinner at a hotel are wanted."* York Courant, *June 11, 1897*

fish rod overhanging the tracks, with its copper fish line, connecting with pure soldering to that of the next pole. Its occasional turnouts and suspended network of wires; and beneath all the gracefully "kinked" track, large and awkward frogs and switches. These turnouts, many swell into the narrow road, and prevent that daring character, who daily menaces the public safety by fast driving, from disturbing the peace and quiet of the town.

Should not this disturber of the town's peace, give way to the advance of science and invention, and allow the inhabitants to enjoy the quiet of their homes at all times? Is not the hissing, hissing, rumbling of an electric car much more conducive to home comforts than the rhythmatic beat of horse's hoofs? Will not the hours of rest be increased, by the abolition of the noisy vacationist, who visits the town with his "best" girl in a side-car box buggy and the introduction of the noiseless (?) trolley with its freight of 50 or 75 best girls and cavaliers?

Will it now be a livening scene, to watch the gambols of 50 or 75 car loads of such enthusiastic visitors, over the fields and rocks? What a delightful picture to paint for the lover of a quiet summer resort. Why haven't such methods been used before to add to the list of summer guests?

What must be provided to entertain this great influx of summer boarders? A dance hall with a violin, clarinet and piano, jingling out spasms of "My girl is a high born lady." The regular boarder watches the dancers with their hands clasped and arms rigidly outstretched square from the shoulder with movements similar to a horse with the blind-staggers. The watcher is highly entertained with this exhibition and wonders if this is the constant attraction?

Those who do not dance cannot be entertained this way, so they try the "swings," some the "flying horses" and some test their lungs to see how much they can "blow." The steam caliope discourses sweet music to call the attention to "the only genuine original life-size bust" of the latest criminal, also the thrilling pictures of terrible carnage in battles in Greece, by their special artists.

How edifying and instructive. Notice the fearless wonder of the regular summer boarder, who gazes with open mouth and asks "where he is at?" After due deliberation he notifies his business friends in Boston or New York, that old York has out-done Coney Island. This is just what a businessman wants for his tired brain and overtaxed nerves. His usual months vacation will probably be extended to six weeks, to insure a more thorough recuperation at this Mecca for the searchers for rest.

Those who become physically unable to properly operate their pedal organs, must be looked after to prevent the refined visitor from interfering with the uncertain progress of this "hilarious stranger." The railroad will do this to show its gratitude for the surrender of the streets. If it becomes too costly for the railroad to rid the town of these muddled visitors, it may appoint and support a judge for trials, and run its own house of correction.

There can be one effect of an electric road between a city and a country town; the natural trend of business is surely toward the city. It is astonishing to see the interest shown by the merchants of York in this electric road scheme, for they are the ones who will be injured by the thing. York Courant, *July 23, 1897*

This is truly what York needs to complete the reputation she has long held as an aristocratic summer resort.

The "anti-trollyites" must certainly be wrong not to see the great gain York is to make by the introduction of the trolley system.

They are to be pitied for their wisdom for it is not appreciated and they, like the prophet, "are without honor in their own country."

But, seriously, they know what they are talking about.

OBSERVER

Miss Pickering's House in York Harbor. It was on the site of what is now Moulton Park. Courtesy of Frank Parsons.

The Varrell House and Annex in York Harbor. Courtesy of Eleanor Fry.

York Beach

The officers of the electric railroad have decided to make the termination of their railroad at present near the Atlantic House and will build a waiting room for their patrons.

The Electric Railroad

York Harbor is fighting the introduction of electric cars and it is declared the residents propose to sue for damages if the road is built. Of course they will have to show that they have sustained damages and in this way the public may be able to get a little definite information as to the actual damage the introduction of such modern improvements really does to a secluded resort. The information will be valuable.

Three More Suits

Three more suits were entered against the Portsmouth and York Electric Railroad yesterday afternoon and still the work of building the line is moving along at a lively rate. Had the weather been fair all day, the rails would have been laid through the entire length of the disputed territory. The rain today interfered with the progress of the work.

May 21, 1897

Communication

As "Hotel" and property owners of York, we wish to make a protest against such articles as appear over the signature of "Observer."

Not wishing to discuss the merits for or against the Electric R.R., we do protest and fail to see where such sarcastic and unjust remarks, appearing just before the arrival of summer boarders, can possibly do anyone any good, while it can do irreparable injury to every hotel and cottage owner in York.

We should guard very carefully all published statements relative to the attractive or unattractive conditions existing. One word said against a summer resort has more effect than twenty for it. As a matter of business, refrain "Observer."   F.A. Ellis & Co. OCEAN HOUSE

Hillcroft Inn before the porches were enclosed.

York Street as it passed by Norwood Farms in York Harbor.

Off For the Battlefield

Edward S. Marshall of the Marshall House, York Harbor, Geo. A. Marshall, Hon. Edward C. Moody, John E. Staples, Capt. Leander Donnell, Daniel A. Stevens, Abraham Vermule of the Passaconaway Inn, and several other prominent residents of York arrived in this city by the early train from York Beach this morning to take passage for Alfred. They plan to attend the hearing before Judge Wiswall on the petition for a restraining order against the Portsmouth, Kittery and York Electric Railroad Company. Besides this delegation, a party left York at an early hour in a six-horse barge for Alfred on the same errand. Whether their efforts have any other effect or not, the York opponents of the electric road will undoubtedly be able to convince the judge that they are very much in earnest in their opposition to the road.

New Hotel

The Iduna Spring Hotel Co. to Erect a Fine Hotel Immediately on the Donnell House Site.

Work has commenced and is being pushed on a hotel which is to be completed by July in time for business this season.

It is being built on the site of the Donnell House which was destroyed by fire last October.

The new hotel will have four stories built on a modern plan, lighted by electricity and will be conducted as a family hotel. It will accommodate about 130 guests. The Iduna Spring water, which by analysis has proved to be one of the purest waters in the world, will be furnished to guests free while stopping at the hotel. The Iduna Spring Hotel Co. are the proprietors.

Have the Electrics Struck Another Snag?

Rumor says that in 1776 the Rices obtained a charter for a ferry across Portsmouth River and the business was carried on until 1820 when they sold out to the Portsmouth Bridge Co. At this time the bridge company obtained a charter for the bridge, with the provision that no further ferrying could be carried out within one mile of said bridge.

Now it is claimed that this will stop the electric railroad company from running their proposed ferry there. At any rate there seems to be lots of things in the way of the electrics.

News and Notes

Fifty-six Italians arrived on Wednesday.

A vessel loaded with piling arrived at York Harbor, Thursday. It will be used in the construction of the electric railroad bridge.

Our Records

In the testimony of the Town Clerk Allen C. Moulton at Alfred before Judge Wiswell in the electric railroad case, he testified that the town records from 1874 to 1888 cannot be found. This is a rather serious statement for a clerk to make under oath. Of course there is no blame attached to Mr. Moulton, as the records were missing before he entered the service as clerk. Something should be done in this matter and these records, which are priceless, should be placed where they belong. The courts should be enjoined in the search if need be.

May 28, 1897

Kittery Point

There was considerable driving on Sunday, many going along the route of the electric road.

The rails for the electric R.R. are being laid from near E.A. Talpey's store to York Village, thence to Portsmouth.

York Harbor Road Wins

Judge Wiswell, in an interview with the Globe's representative this afternoon, said regarding his decree of refusal to grant a temporary injunction against the York Harbor electric railroad:

"The statement to the effect that the complaintants had appealed to the law court to be held at Augusta, Thursday, is incorrect, because so far as the petition for a temporary injunction is concerned, my decision not to grant one is final, and from it there can be no appeal. The managers of the Portsmouth, Kittery and York Electric Railroad may go ahead and construct their line, knowing, however, that a petition for a permanent injunction may be made and may be heard by the law court, a jury of seven judges, to be convened at Portland in July.

Knowing this, the managers work entirely on their own responsibility, relying on the decision of the law court being favorable to them."

The road intends to do this, and have the line running by July 1. (Globe, May 25.)

News and Notes

Several Italians had a row at the Beach, Saturday over a shovel.

Ye Italians don't like the rainy weather as they cannot work on the electric road.

Only twenty-eight working days to July 1st. Can they build the electrics in that time?

Case Gone to Law Court

Full Bench of Maine to Decide the York Harbor Question

J.T. Davidson of York, counsel for the Y.H.&B. railroad, denies the report that the Supreme Court of Maine has decided the injunction case in favor of the Portsmouth, Kittery & York Electric Railroad. He says that no such decision has yet been made.

On the contrary, Judge Wiswell at the Alfred Court last Saturday refused to decide the questions which are involved in this case until they could be submitted to the full bench, or law court, which is composed of seven judges. Judge Wiswell indicated that the questions involved were too serious for a single justice to decide, so the case goes to the July law term.

The dispatch which appeared in Sunday's Globe was based on a message which was received by Hon. Horace Mitchell from Manager A.F. Gerald of the Portsmouth, Kittery and York Electric Railroad. It read, "Injunction denied—all other suits withdrawn except water company—and that postponed."

One Record Found

The book of town records for 1874 to 1888 has been found after an absence of many years.

The Village people have not been slow to accuse one of the Harbor people with having hidden these records, so that the bounds of the Harbor road might not be found during the heated fight over the electric railroad. Now the book has been found in the possession of Wilson M. Walker, Esq. at the Village. It seems that when the bank vaults were opened for the reception of valuables a few years ago, Mr. Walker put some of his books therein and with them this record book. It is rather a curious thing that the book should turn up now the fight is over, and it is more curious that the book was in his possession.

June 4, 1897

Kittery Point

Hon. Horace Mitchell made a flying trip to Washington D.C., last week on business connected with the electric railroad.

Kittery

A pile driver and raft of piling has been towed up Chauncey's Creek to build the electric road bridge that crosses the creek near the old mill dam at Cutts Island.

There is much speculation as to whether the electric road will be completed by the first of July. The projectors still maintain that it will be, but the force of workmen must be greatly increased and the weather more favorable than it has been for the past week.

BOSTON AND MAINE OBJECTS

Opposing Building Overhead Bridge for Electric Road at Y.H.

An interesting hearing was held in Augusta, before the railroad commissioners on the petition of the Portsmouth, Kittery and York Railway for a right to cross the York Harbor and Beach Railroad.

J.T. Davidson of York, appeared as attorney for the Boston & Maine Railroad, which operates the York Harbor and Beach railroad. He opposed permitting the electric railway to build a bridge over the York Harbor and Beach railroad because the construction would interfere with the summer travel of the steam road.

Mr. Gerald stated that the contracts guaranteed the building of the road by July 1.

Hon. H.M. Heath, the attorney for the electric roads, contended for the chartered rights of the road, urging that no action be taken to retard the work now in progress. No decision was given by the commissioners.

June 11, 1897

Kittery Point

Work on the electric road is being rushed. Another lot of Italians arrived last Friday, which, in addition to those already here, make a large gang. The car house is nearly completed and the power house in nearly ready for the roof. The boilers for the latter are expected daily.

The bridge across Chauncey's Creek near Cutts Island, is nearly completed.

Henry A. Marden has gone to Boston to look after the ferry to be used by the electric road. It is now lying at the wharf in that city.

York

The town of York, by its selectmen should compel the electric road magnates to put flat rails instead of T-rails through the compact part of town—Say to them, "gentlemen, put in flat rails or none, as you please"— and stand by it.

Communication

Mr. Editor:

The proper subject for discussion in York today seems to be the electric R.R. versus B.&M.R.R. and monopoly. Monopoly today is one of the many curses of this fair land. It gives to those only with large capital, fine cottages, a span of horses with fine equipage and liveried servants, the privilege of enjoying the beauties of York.

To the laboring man with his little family who wishes for an outing of a day, it says: "Keep Out, this is no place for you, we don't want you with your lunch basket; only those who are able to pay $1.50 for a dinner at a hotel are wanted."

The writer was born in old York and lived there for twenty years. In those days it was a free country. No monopoly. All well-behaved people were welcomed to come and go.

I propose in August to visit the old homestead for a day, and bring a

A Briggs open car crossing Norton's Trestle from York Village to York Harbor. Courtesy of O.R. Cummings.

The disputed trestle across the York Harbor & Beach Railroad at Seabury in York.

lunch basket of indigestible food. I shall ride on the electrics because it costs less.

Now to whom shall I apply for permission to enter old York, with my lunch basket?

The B.&M. or to some Nabob who says he owns all the rights and titles to that fair land, even to the air we breathe?

Those high bloods with more money than brains, where did their money come from?

Was it not largely from the class of people they are trying to keep out?

I am glad to see the electrics going into old York, and giving the lunch basket crowd a chance to visit the ancient city of Gorgeana.

LUNCH BASKET

News and Notes

Civil Engineer Libby and his assistant, Clarence Gaines, of Saco were in town early in the week. They were making surveys of the Harbor relative to widening the street, to accommodate the electric railroad.

Mr. Gerald, the manager of the electric road, was the first person to meet with an accident on the road. Being at the Harbor on Tuesday, his wagon wheel caught in the track and twisted every spoke out of the wheel. No further damage. This is only a foretaste of what the people of York and her visitors have got to take.

Owing to a washout on the B.&M. line near Seabrook, the Y.H.&B. Train was an hour and a half late Thursday noon.

June 25, 1897

Correspondents

York Village

Last week while unloading railroad ties at the Harbor, Mr. W.H. Grant jammed off the top of the middle finger of his left hand. An Italian working with him having some knowledge of surgery, treated the wound in a scientific manner and later on it was treated by Dr. Cook.

Interior of a St. Louis 30′ closed car. Courtesy of O.R. Cummings.

Passengers anxiously waiting for the trolley at the Bald Head Cliff station.

News & Notes

The existence and location of that Kittery electric line is certainly being well advertised – *Biddeford Times*.

Yes, and we should say that so much advertising of this character might tend to injure the sale of the proposed bonds.

Up to the hour of going to press no decision has been reached relative to the removal of the rails of the electric road from York Harbor streets.

See the new time table for the Y.H.&B. R.R. Don't imagine for a moment that the old one is correct.

Iduna Spring Hotel is fast being pushed to completion.

On Tuesday as Mr. Charles Oscar Trafton was driving one of G. Frank Austin's two horse teams, loaded with poles, down a hill at Kittery Point. A bolt in the pole broke, causing the horses to run and throw him from the load. Mr. Trafton narrowly escaped being run over by the wheels but was considerably shaken up and injured in the shoulders and ankle. The team was stopped without any further serious damage.

An Injunction On

It is not generally known, but the reason for the delay in building the bridge for the electric railroad between Badger's Island and Kittery was because of an injunction placed against it by the government.

It seems that some one wrote to Washington stating that the ships' channel was being obstructed by the bridge, and the authorities decided to put an injunction on building the bridge.

July 2, 1897

Kittery Point

Part of the rolling stock for the electric road has arrived and has been conveyed to the car house.

Entrance to the P.K.&Y. carhouse at Kittery Point. Courtesy of Hugh Dunston.

PORTSMOUTH, KITTERY AND YORK ELECTRIC RAILROAD

July 9, 1897

News and Notes

Warren Keen of Portsmouth will have charge of construction of the new overhead bridge to be built by the Electric R.R. Co. at Seabury.

It is said that the cigars required to pay the bets of a certain newspaper man in Portsmouth on the running of the electric cars by July 4, would probably load the first car that does run.

This road, if built, will probably cross the Kennebunk River on the new draw bridge at Kennebunkport. An electric railroad now runs from Portsmouth to York and this one would probably connect with it there. It would make a splendid ride along the shore for nearly fifty miles, with the ocean constantly in sight. It is very doubtful if it would be a good thing for either Kennebunk Beach or Kennebunkport, as it would bring in a class of transient excursionists who would destroy rather than benefit the place.

The Iduna Spring Hotel

In forty-four working days the Iduna Spring Hotel has been built from the forest and dinner served therein on Tuesday. This house is 125 feet front, four story and has been built, finished and furnished in the above named time, which we think is "pretty quick dodging."

York Beach

J.Q. Adams is at work with his team for the Electric R.R. Co.

Kittery Point

The freight yard at the depot has been the center of attraction for large numbers since last Friday, when two of the electric cars arrived. They are of the open pattern, ten seats and like the ordinary cars run in the large cities. They are painted and lettered in good style and will be taken to the car house this week. The front of the car house has lately been lettered and is a fine piece of work. It was done by Fred Harraden, one of the best sign painters in Portsmouth.

The exterior of the depot and freight house are being brightened by a coat of paint and will be the same color as the railroad buildings on the main line.

An open car crossing the York River on Sewall's bridge. Courtesy of Cynthia Hayes.

An open car passing through York Village c. 1915.

News and Notes

The owners of the big steam pile driver at Kittery have been drawing $54 per day and up to Thursday only 10 piles had been driven.

A long line of cottages on Long Beach still display the legend "to let," and with not very brilliant prospects of occupancy.

New Slip Located

All the work put in the past week on the Badger's Island slip of the electric ferry has gone for naught. A ledge was encountered some distance from the shore which defied all attempts made at pile driving. After spoiling half a dozen red oak piles, the attempt was abandoned.

The only thing left to do was to locate the slip farther up the stream. A new deal was made with William Willey, owner of the property, to construct the slip off the end of this wharf. Mr. Willey was paid $36 per year for 25 years and given a pass on the ferry.

July 23, 1897

The Electric Railroad

The editor of this paper has reasonable chance, and doubtless a fighting chance, to say a few words upon the question of the electric railroad.

We have no axe to grind; no friend to please; no enemy to spite. The electric has its charter and thereby its franchise. We do not deny those rights, yet while we might reasonably criticize the action of the projectors in their location (and as firmly believe they have made a fatal error, which time will well develop) we of course bow to their better judgement.

We have friends upon both sides of this question, but we do not feel inclined to leave our opinion in doubt.

As to the value of the road to the town we believe it to be on a par with a circus. However, the circus is "for one day only," while the road is continuous. The circus carries out more dollars — ten to one, than it brings into any town.

The settled inhabitants are aware of the fact that certain of them go to Portsmouth even now, ostensibly to save a few cents on the price of certain goods. The real fact of their going, is to "fill their tank" "treat their friends," and "bring home a quart for the next day."

Trolley cars eventually replaced the stage coaches which provided local transportation in the resort areas. Courtesy of Mr. and Mrs. Charles Main.

The Iduna Spring Hotel on Long Beach.

Now brother Gerald told us in town meeting that "you people will ride four times as much with a low fare as you do now." Admit this as a fact and lets see the result. The man goes to Portsmouth four times when once would do; he spends four times as much of valuable time in Portsmouth as he spends now; he treats four times as many friends; he drinks or eats four times as much as he would now; he spreads four times as much ruin upon the home circle as he would now; and he becomes the four times besotted sot that he is now. This applies to one class only but how about the other? It is characteristic of human nature to go farther to buy that which they can buy at home as well. Your lady who wants a yard of ribbon, or your dude who wants a hat will take the electrics for Portsmouth, as the Portsmouth people go to Boston, the Boston people go to New York, and the New Yorkites go to Paris for styles.

We ask our readers if our theory is not correct? There can be one effect of an electric road between a city and a country town; the natural trend of business is surely toward the city. It is astonishing to see the interest shown by the merchants of York in this electric road scheme, for they are the ones who will be injured by the thing.

We believe that this scheme will be the greatest calamity that ever struck York, but are disposed to "await a while with patience."

Grand Ball

Reception and Dance of the Season at the Iduna Spring Hotel.

The management of the Iduna Spring Hotel at Long Beach has decided to dedicate the fine new building August 10, with a brilliant ball to surpass anything ever given at York before. The dancing and promenading capacity of the Iduna is about 8000 feet. It is lighted with electricity and for this occasion its broad piazzas will be specially luminated and decorated.

It is so arranged that the whole lower floor can be turned into one magnificent dance hall. The ball will be preceded by an orchestral concert and followed by a banquet.

Day's well-known orchestra of Worcester has been engaged for the season by the Iduna. Lovers of dancing understand what this means. Reception committees are now being formed.

Kittery Point

Workmen were engaged on Sunday in unloading and conveying two of the electric cars from the railroad station to the car house. They were of the eight wheel pattern, fourteen seats, and will seat seventy persons. They are forty feet ten inches in length, the same size as the cars that run on the Nantasket Beach line of the NYNH&H Railroad. We are assured that the cars will be running by August 1st.

Capt. Henry Marden, who has been in Boston looking after the electric ferry, is passing a few days at home, as he is not obliged to stay aboard the craft since she arrived from Boston. Large numbers went to Badger's Island on Sunday to see something that many had never seen — a ferry.

A watchman is now stationed at the carhouse nights to look after the property. There are now six cars there and most of them all ready to run. The lineman wired the inside on Sunday and the telephone company has installed a telephone.

VIATOR in the Portsmouth Times says "In consequence of the tearing up of the roads at the Harbor the highways were considerably damaged, but the railroad corporation purchased gravel from the town of York, and has rendered the roads in a better condition than what they ever were before."

With all due deference to "VIATOR," we don't think so. The road at York Harbor was in better condition prior to its being torn up by the electric people, than it has been since, or will for a long time again be.

The excursion train from Boston Tuesday brought quite a large number of people into town. Most of them dined at the Yorkshire and business was lively there for about three hours.

Fred W. Marshall has entered the employ of the Portsmouth, Kittery and York Electric Railroad at the power house.

August 6, 1897

"Its too funny for anything" when our legislature passes a law making an Arbor day, and the governor appoints a day annually as such, and the people of the state set out shade and other ornamental trees, and then the legislature gives to some soul-less electric road corporation full authority to cut and slash and destroy any and all of said trees that come in their way. Here in old York, they go out of their way to do this.

The electrics, in arranging for their feed wire were passing the

PORTSMOUTH, KITTERY AND YORK ELECTRIC RAILROAD 53

The Kittery Point carhouse and power station was built in 1897.

The ferry Kittery *at the Badger's Island landing. Courtesy of O.R. Cummings.*

Ferry landing and waiting room on Badger's Island, Kittery, Maine.

Portsmouth ferry landing.

elegant residence of S.W. Junkins Esq. They decided it was necessary to destroy the splendid shade trees in front of his premises.

Mr. Junkins has prudently called the attention of the Selectmen to the fact that the electric people have no right to pass over that road, as it is not on the line of their track.

The counsel for the road, Mr. Heath, was consulted by the Selectmen and he informs them that Mr. Junkins is correct. This is another of the many snags the electrics have met. There is however a bigger one ahead than any yet.

Kittery Point

Another car for the electric road arrived Monday. It has two steps, and is quite an improvement over the ones now set up.

The First Car

The first electric car of the Kittery and York Electric Railroad Company crossed the bridge onto Badger's Island on Wednesday morning at 10:30 o'clock.

On board were officials of the road and many prominent citizens of Kittery. The car stopped on the bank in plain view from this side of the river. The ferry boat whistle was the first to announce the approach of the car. Then the river steamers took up the call and saluted loudly.

After a short stop the car was run back to the power station.

Correspondence

Kittery Point

With the opening of the electric road and the visit of the White Squadron, the past week has been a busy one and the place is full of strangers. The hotels have been full and in some cases have had to hire rooms in nearby cottages. Every boat that could be used was pressed into service to convey people to the ships, and the regular steamers have done a large business. All day Friday and Saturday the electrics were crowded and many had to stand....

Charles Sawyer has accepted the position of purser on the electric ferry. Capt. Sawyer is a thorough sailor and will prove a very hardy man at the wheel as well as ticket taker.

Hon. I.C. Libby of the electric road, who with his pleasant family are summering at the Hotel Champernowne, have made many friends during their stay here.

There is some talk of making a park and picnic grounds at Sea Point. The fine sandy beach is nearly a quarter of a mile long. It is hard enough to drive heavy teams over, and would make an ideal place for picnics as it is on the line of the electric road.

York Beach

The excursion from New Hampshire last week was one of the most successful of the season. The train consisted of twelve cars in which 657 people were transported to this popular seaside resort. The party included a good representation of the best residents in the towns along the Suncook Valley and Manchester and North Ware branches. The day was a delightful one, and everyone was delighted with Maine's popular seaside resort.

The electric wire has been put in place from its terminus to York Harbor, and the road is nearly ready for the cars. People are anxiously waiting for a ride over the new road.

The Iduna Spring Hotel is lighted with electric lights from Marshall's plant, which is a great improvement over the old way of lighting.

August 27, 1897

Scotland

We are pleased to learn that Melvin McIntire, of Brixham is one of the conductors on the Kittery and York electric road.

Kittery Road

The steamers have reduced the fare between here and Portsmouth, and are doing a good business, notwithstanding the electric cars. The trip on the steamer is a pleasant one, and many prefer it to the electrics.

York Beach

The illumination promises to be the great event of the season. The managers of the electric road and the committee are doing all they can to make the illumination of 1897 the greatest demonstration York Beach has ever seen.

September 3, 1897

York Harbor

Golf and various informal gatherings at the cottages have been the major social happenings here this week. Now that the electric cars have really arrived, those who have heretofore enjoyed the pleasant drives in this vicinity find that they literally have their hands full with their spirited horses. All this only adds to the popularity of golf, and the average cottager contents himself with the reflection that the summer is almost over, and that the bicycles and boats do not shy at electric cars. The streets have been left in fairly good condition, and the tracks filled with earth and leveled off in quilt-edged fashion. This is not the case with the rest of the route, a fine tribute to the efficacy of complaint, which the natives of surrounding towns should heed. At any rate, the denizens of neighboring towns and summer settlements are enjoying their view of this erstwhile quiet and aristocratic village. They enjoy the electric cars, with the exception of those brief moments when the cars pass over York's "Frankenstein Trestles" near the railroad, and everyone is busy wondering if the bridges are strong enough.

Editorial

The first electric car crossed Sewall's Bridge on Thursday afternoon at about 4.15 P.M. We rode to the residence of Mrs. Mercer, near York Harbor. This was a free ride. We then rode back to Sewall's Bridge, which was also free. Then we took the regular electric for Portsmouth. On this trip we met one of the town officers who was surprised to see us on the car. We are happy to say that the ride to Portsmouth was indeed very pleasant and in fact beautiful. The conducters were gentle and affable men, as of course they were supposed to be. Manager Gerald was on the "trial trip," and was overflowing with genial good nature, as is his custom. All of our previous remarks have been made upon principles in

Extending the trolley car line to St. Aspinquid Park. Courtesy of Norman Chase.

Entrance to St. Aspinquid Park which had a restaurant, menagerie, dance hall and picnic grounds.

which we believed. We have no ill feelings against any man. We have expressed our opinion as we think we had a good right to do, and were conscientious in our statements. That the road is here, we know. Whether it is a matter of permanency, we do not know. The road is now doing a flattering business, but we wonder what the dreary months of December and January will bring. We do know that the road will be of great benefit to Portsmouth.

We can only hope for the best, and accept the inevitable, as all men are obliged to do. The officers of the road are gentlemen in every sense of the word, and have handled the extensive business of the work in first class shape. We wish the road all the success due for the indefatigable efforts of the promoters.

Portsmouth and York Beach Railroad

Facts and figures about the New Electric Road. Doing a Good Business.

Hon. I.C. Libby who has built the Portsmouth and York Beach railroad gives the following figures showing what has been earned each day up to Tuesday. It was opened as far as Kittery Point Aug. 13. On that day it received in fares $200; on each of the following days up to the 27th, the earnings were as follows: $171, $215, $200, $57, $94, $102, $110. Sunday 22nd., $220, $177, $47.75, $200, $160.

On Friday the 27th, the road commenced carrying passengers to York Beach and received in fares on that day $475; on Saturday they took $600; Sunday more than $800, the exact figures could not be ascertained. This shows that the people were only waiting for a chance to ride as soon as somebody would furnish the road to do it.

Mr. Libby is a hustler, and was engaged in the cattle business for thirty years before he began building electric roads. He says many of those who oppose his building this road are now patronizing and praising it, and cannot understand why they opposed the building of it.

Mr. Libby talked quite freely of his plans for the future. They intend soon to have two powerful ferryboats running across the river to carry the passengers back and forth. One of these boats will gather the passengers from the landings along the shores of Newcastle as far as where the Government boat lands. The other will touch the landings above there so that people will not have to go to one particular wharf to be carried across the river.

A trolley car at the Goldenrod in York Beach, c.1910. Courtesy of the Goldenrod.

Interior of the Goldenrod before the porch was added. Courtesy of the Goldenrod.

They have taken measurements of the depth of the water in the river from the landing at Badger's Island across to the old brick church, and found the bottom is a ledge all the way. The shores have deep water close up, at the deepest point the water at ordinary high tide is 75 feet. There is no mud on the bottom because the tide cleans it out every day. Mr. Libby says it is practicable to put a bridge across there. It would be fastened solid to the ledge bottom, and that they propose to take steps at the meeting of the next legislatures of Maine and New Hampshire to ask for an appropriation of $40,000 from each state. The electric road will furnish the rest of the capital which he estimates at $200,000, to build a free bridge for the electric road and the general public. He predicts this will be accomplished early in the next century.

September 10, 1897

Electric Railroad Talk

The talk of an electric railroad to connect East Rochester, Rochester and Dover, is being renewed. A.F. Gerald, Pres. of the Portsmouth, Kittery, and York road, has looked over this field and says that it is one of the best openings for the successful operation of an electric road in this part of New England.

The opening of an electric road will lengthen the season at York, which for the past month has been a busy place indeed. All through October many of the cottages will be occupied. No place along the coast excels the Nubble for sea fowl shooting, a fact fully recognized by sportsmen far and near. The delightful ride will be enjoyed by many until late in the fall.

Scotland

Sunday, David McIntire, 78 years old, rode on the electric cars. It was the first time he ever saw an electric car.

Kittery Point

The motormen and conductors on the electric road as a rule are very accommodating and polite men. One of the conductors is James Hogan, a neat and civil young man from Bath. Mr. Hogan came here

The LaFayette Inn was renamed The Breakers. After the hotel burned, it was replaced by the Sands Motel.

before the road was opened and was night watchman at the car house for some time. It is hoped by many that when the winter service goes into effect, which will probably mean the laying off of several men, that "Jimmy" may remain in his present position.

The electric road was slightly handicapped last week by the water supply giving out. This difficulty was surmounted by sending to Portsmouth for a street sprinkler, with which they conveyed water from nearby wells to the power station. The source of supply is Deerings Ice Pond, which will be deepened. It is thought that when this is done there will be no danger of a water shortage even in the dryest season of the year.

News and Notes

The electric railroad did another big days' business on Sunday and every car to and from the Beach was crowded.

The Portsmouth, Kittery and York Street Railway Co. is having the electric poles painted.

Electric Road Fares

For the benefit of the York people we give the revised limit for collecting fares on the electric road:

Portsmouth to Emery Place at Kittery, including ferry	5cts.
Emery Place to Thaxter's	5cts.
Thaxter's to Seabury Station	5cts.
Seabury Station to York Harbor	5cts.
York Harbor to York Beach	5cts.
	25cts.

Previous to Wednesday the limit has been Sewall's Bridge instead of Seabury Station. The change was made for the accommodation of people who live along the road this side of Sewall's bridge, and do business in York.

A special ticket is being prepared to enable patrons at York Village to ride to York Beach for five cents. People at York Beach can ride to York Village for five cents by purchasing these tickets which will be on sale at each of the places.

September 17, 1897

News and Notes

Last week, Mr. & Mrs. Samuel Blake of Kittery Point, went to York Beach on an electric car. Mrs. Blake had not visited the Beach for fifty-five years, and it was the first time she ever rode on a car of any kind.

The Fairmont has registered 461 people from Sept. 1st to Sept. 15th.

Yorkshire Inn has forty-three guests and will not close until October.

Safe Blown Open

Sometime last night the passenger station at Long Beach was broken into and the safe blown open and $50 in money taken. Entrance was gained by forcing two doors. The charge of powder was so heavy as to completely demolish the safe and wreck the woodwork about it.

September 24, 1897

Vestibule Cars Arrive

Two new electric cars arrived Tuesday for the Portsmouth, Kittery and York street railway. They are of the latest improved pattern. An aisle runs down the center of the cars and seats are arranged in pairs on either side. The motorman is entirely closed in, protecting him from all kinds of weather.

It is the determination of the managers to make this one of the best equipped roads in the country. The enclosed cars are to be put on the rails sometime this week.

Kittery Point

Under the direction of Supt. Meloon of the electric road, they have built a car differing in some respects from the ones now running on the road. This car resembles the ordinary flat car used on steam roads with the exception of the trolley pole, which is supported by a large upright made of iron pipe, securely fastened to the floor of the car. The wires from the motor to the trolley are inside this pipe. This car is a four wheeler, fitted with motors, brakes, controllers and gong. It will be used to convey rails, poles, gravel and anything needed in the construction of the road. It will save considerable freighting by teams. The closed cars are said to be on the way here and they will be very welcome these cold mornings and evenings.

York Beach

The electric cars are well patronized. Quite a number of our young people are attending the high school at York Corner, going and returning on the electric cars.

To The Editor

Mr. Editor:

Some of our good people have been worrying about the "cheap trash" and dregs of society that the electrics would bring and dump in our midst, much to the detriment of the morals of our good old puritanic

PORTSMOUTH, KITTERY AND YORK ELECTRIC RAILROAD

A double truck flatcar followed by a locomotive.

town. However, all we can see are respectable people riding on the electrics, as on the steam cars; and besides, there does seem to be something really electric about the electrics. Only a few days ago, they brought two of our fair cousins from the country, aged eighty-five and eighty-seven. They came twenty miles to ride on the electrics, and as soon as they got off, began to joke with each other about the "fellows." There is no telling how many "mashes" they made during their stay, but, there's no doubt that Cupid's dart found deep enlodgement in the heart of some bald-headed swain. At any rate we were glad to see them and when the electrics bore them away, our eyes moistened, and we said, "God bless the old girls," the electric cars have done them, and us, a good deal of good.

A New Car Barn

The managers of the Portsmouth, Kittery and York electric road are to erect a large car shed at York Beach. The shed is to be 40×90 feet. The site has not been decided upon at present but negotiations are going on for the purchase of a lot of land on this side of York Beach.

October 1, 1897

Surveying for Electrics

S.W. Junkins Esq., is now engaged in making preliminary surveys for the electric road people, commencing at the York Beach terminus. Two routes are being surveyed, one by way of Bald Head and one by the post road via Cape Neddick Village to Ogunquit Village.

The road will be built in the spring.

Kittery Point

The cars are proving very convenient for persons wishing to attend the plays or visit Portsmouth in the evening. A number of Masons attended a meeting there on Monday evening to witness the degree of Master Mason worked by the Past Masters of St. Andrews Lodge, F.&A.M.

The new closed cars are all right, and we don't have to undergo the pleasure of having our toes trodden on as we do in the ordinary closed cars.

York Beach

Our people are well pleased with the beautiful and convenient cars the electric railroads are furnishing their patrons these cold days. They are an improvement over the old style. To appreciate their beauty and comfort one must take a ride.

E.A. Talpey is doing a rushing business in his line since the electric cars stop near his place. It's an ill wind that blows no one any good.

Electric Car Stations

The Portsmouth, Kittery and York electric road has established car stations at the following stores along the line, where tickets may be obtained, as well as information concerning running times of cars, ferry, etcs.:

Kittery Foreside-W.T. Spinney
Kittery Point-T. Clarkson & Son
York Village-W.M. Walker

York Harbor – D.A. Stevens
York Beach – E.A. Talpey

Closed cars leave Ferry Station, Badger's Island on the even hour; leave York Beach on the half hour.

Stoned the Car

Thursday evening, conductor Thomas Wilson, who is in charge of one of the electric cars, had considerable trouble with a couple of Frenchmen while on his way to York. At last the men got so "fresh" that the car was stopped and the conductor, with the help of the motorman, put them off. Upon starting off again both men stoned the car until it was out of reach.

A warrant was made out for their arrest Thursday and authorities are engaged in looking for them.

Magnates Meet

Messrs. A.F. Gerald of Fairfield, Me., I.C. Libbey of Waterville, Me., H.B. Goodenough, Bridgeton, Me., Gilman C. Moses and F.H. Twitchell, Bath, Mr. E.J. Lawrence and S.A. Nye, Fairfield, Me., were in town Tuesday.

These gentlemen compose the syndicate who constructed the Kittery and York electric road. In Kittery they held a meeting and talked over many matters.

It was voted to have the Newmarch converted into a double-ended propeller ferryboat and put in first class condition. The matter of building the road on the Portsmouth side of the river was discussed and work will be commenced in the spring.

The earnings of the road to date amounts to $14,000. One half of this was used in operating the road.

York Beach

The electric railroad company is building a car house near Charles Bowden's. Some of their cars will be left at this end of their line.

News and Notes

The railroad commissioners went over the electric road Wednesday in a special car.

Frank A. Moulton met with a serious accident at the new car stable of the Electric Car Co., at York Beach on Wednesday. He fell twenty-five feet from a staging. John Stover was on the same staging but escaped serious injury.

October 22, 1897

Change of Time

Portsmouth, Kittery and York street railway, in effect Oct. 14, 1897; until further notice cars will run as follows:

Leave Badgers for York Beach–7:00, 8:00, 9:00, 10:00, 11:00, 12:00 A.M. 1:00, 2:00, 3:00, 4:00, 5:00, 6:00, 7:00, 8:00, 9:00, 10:00, 11:00 P.M.

For Sea Point–6:30, 7:30, 8:30, 9:30, 10:30, 11:30 A.M. 12:30, 1:30, 2:30, 3:30, 4:30, 5:30, 6:30 P.M. Saturday evenings only 7:30, 8:30, 9:30.

Leave York Beach for Portsmouth–6:30, 7:30, 8:30, 9:30, 10:30, 11:30 A.M. 12:30, 1:30, 2:30, 3:30, 4:30, 5:30, 6:30, 7:30, 8:30, 9:30, 10:30 P.M.

To Kittery Point only – the 10:00 and 11:00 P.M. cars leaving Badger's Island and the 10:30 from York Beach can be chartered to run through by making application to the Office on Congress Street or at the power station.

Sunday Time same as week except the first car leaves Badger's Island at 8 A.M. and York Beach at 8:30.

Y.H.&B.R.R.

Thursday, the train leaving Portsmouth at 11:10 A.M. carried only three passengers, all of whom got off at York Harbor, and all of them were dead heads. Now gentlemen directors, we say to you in language that you cannot misinterpret; you must do something to hold your trade from the electrics, or you will be unable to declare a one percent dividend next year. They are pulling everlastingly on your business, and can you wonder why?

You render no reasonable service and charge a big price for what you do render.

Put on some trains! Give your patrons a low figure! Beat the band by playing the drum! Don't be a clam!

October 29, 1897

York Beach

The electric car barn is nearly ready for use and will be occupied in a few days.

A large number of people came on the electric cars Friday and Saturday of last week to see the magnificent surf on the Bluffs. There must have been a heavy storm at sea to cause such a high tide.

E.A. Talpey is making some improvements in his store and station for the benefit of the patrons of the electric railroad. He has put a coat of paint on the floor, which is of a diamond shape.

Kittery

Contractor Comers, who has been building bridges for the P.K. and Y. street railway has completed his labors here and returned to his home in Brunswick.

The electric railway co. is having several waiting rooms built along the line of the road for the convenience of its patrons.

NOTES FROM THE NEWS

THE EXTENSION OF THE PORTSMOUTH, KITTERY AND YORK BEACH RAILROAD TO THE SEA WAS THE SIGNAL FOR THE ILLUMINATION AT YORK BEACH ON FRIDAY NIGHT. LARGE NUMBERS OF PEOPLE WENT OVER IN THE ELECTRICS FROM KITTERY. SPECIAL TRAINS WERE RUN FROM MANCHESTER AND SURROUNDING TOWNS, AND RETURNED AT 11 O'CLOCK, SO THAT PEOPLE FROM PORTSMOUTH, NEW CASTLE AND KITTERY COULD JOIN THE FESTIVITIES. THE SEASON OF 1897 WILL LONG BE MEMORABLE IN THE ANNALS OF PISCATAQUA TOWNS, BECAUSE OF THE INCREASED FACILITIES FOR REACHING THE MOST BEAUTIFUL PLACES AND VIEWING THEIR VARIED ATTRACTIONS. JUST NOW THE GOLDENROD, CLEMATIS AND CARDINAL FLOWER MAKE GORGEOUS THE ROAD AND BROOKSIDE, WHILE THE ASTER AND A RED LEAF OR TWO ARE JUST BEGINNING TO APPEAR. THEY ARE BEAUTIFUL REMINDERS OF THE SUMMER THAT HAS ALMOST GONE. DAME NATURE'S FAREWELL ILLUMINATION, TO SPEED THE PARTING GUEST AND LIGHT THE SUMMER WAYFARER UPON HIS HOMEWARD WAY.

A Laconia 13' open bench car crossing the Badger's Island Trestle. Courtesy of O.R. Cummings.

Large numbers went to Badger's Island on Sunday to see something that many had never seen—a ferry.

York Courant, *July 23, 1897*

A Scenic and Historic Trolley Tour

The following description of a ride on the Portsmouth, Kittery and York Electric Railroad is from an unpublished manuscript written by Leonard Withington in 1908. A former editor of the Newburyport Herald, *Withington apparently prepared the information for an advertising brochure which also included the other routes of the expanded trolley system. We offer the text as a description of what it was like to ride the trolley and we have not edited the manuscript in any way.*

PICTURESQUE PORTSMOUTH-on-the Piscataqua is the starting point of the lines of the Atlantic Shore Railway which traverses that wonderland of scenic beauty and historic romance known as Southern Maine. The old seaport town of New Hampshire is itself worthy of many hours of exploration for there are few cities on the Atlantic seaboard that have preserved so well the atmosphere of Colonial days. The mansions of the Wentworths—governors of the bygone days—the house where Washington danced the minuet with the belles and beaux of Old New Hampshire, old St. John's-by-the-Sea and a hundred other quaint and historic spots are close at hand. But, we are starting on a trolley tour and will hasten down Ceres Street, a few steps from the Parade, and board the ferry steamer "Kittery," which is to bear us across the Piscataqua to the Pine Tree State.

As the steamer leaves her slip, we see behind us old *Strawbery Banke*, named by Captain John Smith and his men from the abundance of strawberries that they found growing there. Upstream may be seen the somewhat unsteady outlines of the *Portsmouth Bridge*, built in 1822 and enlarged when the railroad was built. Beyond rises the huge bulk of the new paper mill. Downstream is the *United States Navy Yard*, known as the Portsmouth Yard, but located in the town of Kittery, Maine. The island on which most of the buildings are situated was purchased in 1806 from Capt. William Dennett for $5,500. In this yard were built the *Kearsarge* and many other famous naval vessels. Its chief fame, however, is as the place where the Treaty of Portsmouth, which terminated the Russo-Japanese War, was signed. The *Conference Building*, marked with suitable tablets, is always open to visitors. The tall structure in the background is the new *Naval Prison* on Seavey's Island. On this island were confined the Spanish prisoners taken at the battle of Santiago.

As we land from the ferry, we step upon historic ground. This is *Badger's Island*, the first navy yard of the United Colonies. Here were built the *Raleigh* and the *America*.

The island received its name from Capt. William Badger, who built a hundred ships here. It is said that he never witnessed a launching until that of his hundredth ship which he named for himself.

Let us now take a car on the left hand track, marked *PORTSMOUTH AND YORK BEACH*. Our way lies largely through historic *Kittery*, the oldest town in Maine. It was originally, with much adjoining territory, called Piscataqua and was settled at the Point in 1623. In 1647, it was incorporated as a Massachusetts Plantation and in 1652 was organized as a town under its present name.

Returning to our journey, we pass along *Newmarch Street*, named for Capt. John Newmarch, Harvard, 1690, first pastor in Kittery. His remains lie in a neglected grave in the clump of oaks which stand in the field opposite the end of the street. Here we turn into *Government Street*, while another line turns to the left on its way to Eliot and Dover. The car climbs *Cottle's Hill* and then runs through that part of Kittery known as the *Foreside*, stopping at the entrance to the *Navy Yard* and passing on the right the handsome *Rice Memorial Library*. Just beyond, we pass the Navy Yard station of the steam railroad and can see on a hill to the right *Traip Academy*, a gift to the town. The car next crosses *Locke's Cove*, and we get a close view of the powder magazines of the Navy Yard and, just beyond, the prison ship *Southerly*. Across the bridge at the right is a little house some distance back from the street. This is the *Whipple Garrison House*, built some 230 years ago. It was originally 34 feet square. General William Whipple, a signer of the Declaration of Independence was born here in 1730.

The trolley car at York Corner. Courtesy of O.R. Cummings.

After passing over *Fort Hill* and *Bridge Hill*, we come to the *Kittery Point Bridge* which spans *Spruce Creek*. Crossing this we enter the oldest part of town. Off to the left as we round the next curve may be seen the *Sparhawk House*, a gift from Sir William Pepperell to his daughter on her wedding day. Also to the left is the *Kittery Point Church* with its ancient parsonage. At our right as we make the next turn is the *Cutts House*, better known as the *Lady Pepperell House*, built by Sir William's widow. Near it is the *old burying ground* which contains many old epitaphs including one written by Browning for the grave of Levi L. Thaxter. The nearby siding is called *Champernowne*, from Capt. Francis Champernowne, the land agent of Mason and Gorges. At the right, the second yellow cottage is the summer residence of *William Dean Howells*, the author, and just beyond is the home of the *Piscataqua Yacht Club*.

At the foot of the slight descent the track makes a detour to the left to avoid the grounds of *Fort McClary*. The spot was the site of the fort built by the elder William Pepperell in 1700 and has been used as a fort during every conflict since that time. It received its present name from Major McClary, a gallant young New Hampshire officer who was killed at the battle of Bunker Hill. The picturesque blockhouse is of compara-

Car arriving at the York Beach waiting station. Courtesy of O.R. Cummings.

tively recent date and the fort is now not in use. We skirt the edge of the harbor, a rendezvous of pleasure craft in the summer season. At the left, on a slight elevation, is a tablet to the memory of the *Pepperells* whose tomb is in the clump of evergreens directly back of the tablet.

At right, opposite the Post Office is the *mansion house* built by the Pepperells in the early part of the 18th century. It was once surrounded by magnificent grounds which reached down to the landing where the first American British general took his barge manned by negro boatmen for Portsmouth. Next, beyond the Pepperell mansion, is the *Bray House*, oldest in Kittery and probably the oldest in Maine. It was built prior to 1660 and Majorie Bray, daughter of its builder, was the bride of the elder Pepperell.

On the summit of the next hill we may see the arms of Sir *Ferdinando Gorges*, fixed to the wall of the residence of George Wasson, author and painter. Rounding *Hutchin's Corner*, we pass the power house and carbarns of the company and then skirt the shore of *Chauncy's Creek* beyond which is *Gerrish Island*, the birthplace of many sea captains. When we cross the next creek we are on *Cutt's Island*, so named from the earliest settlers of Kittery. Near *Sea Point*, on clear days, we may see to the southeast the *Isles of Shoals*. Leaving the siding the car makes its way down the rocky ledges, crosses *Brave Boat Harbor* and plunges into the fragrant woods for the long climb up to the line separating Kittery from the town of York.

The *Town of York* was organized in 1652 but was antedated by ten years by the first city in America. This was the city of Gorgeana established by Sir Ferdinando Gorges, Lord Palatine of Maine, on the banks of the *York River*, originally the Organug and then called the Agamenticus. The first permanent settlement at York was made about 1628 but the coast was discovered by Gosnold in 1602 and explored by others later.

After entering York, the car passes the *Raynes Neck* or *Seabury* schoolhouse and soon emerges from a rocky cut and runs out on the odd *curved trestle* which carries the electric road over the track and the Seabury station of the steam railroad. From this trestle one has a magnificent view of York Harbor with its narrow entrance, Fort Head, the islands connected by the causeway of the new bridge, the hotels and cottages rising on the further shore and the blue Atlantic in the background.

A short distance beyond Seabury is *Hazen's siding*, near the home of ex-governor Rollins of New Hampshire, the father of Old Home Week. Beyond, the car passes through one of the most beautiful bits of woodland to be found on the entire system, skirts the quiet waters of the *York River* and crosses *Sewall's Bridge*. This historic structure was built in 1757 from plans by Major Samuel Sewall and was the first pile draw-bridge in America. If the major had known that modern trolley cars were to pass over his bridge, he would probably have constructed a different sort of draw.

After leaving the bridge, we pass the handsome home of the *York Country Club* and follow Organug Road through the golf links, past the new high school, to the rotary substation of the trolly company at *York Corner*, where connections may be made with the "Cross Country Line" for Eliot, South Berwick and Dover. We now pass through a thickly settled section and, after leaving York Village turnout, soon come to the village green.

The *Village Green* of York is surpassed by few, if any, in New England. In the midst of grounds laid out by expert landscape artists arises the *First Parish Church* crowned by one of the most beautiful spires in existence, and said to have been from a design by Bullfinch. A tablet at the right of the entrance states that the church was erected in

1747 and was extensively repaired in 1882. At the left of the church is the *parsonage* and vestry and at the right is the *Town Hall*, for many years the county court house. Opposite the green, on the right of the track is the *ancient burying ground* and the old *Wilcox Tavern*, now a summer residence. Just beyond the tavern on a hill is the oldest English public building in the United States. This is the *Old Gaol of York*, erected in 1653 and now a museum of colonial and other relics. There is much of interest in this old building and its collections. It is well worth a visit.

As the car stops in front of the post office and bank in the village, we see at the left the road to *York Heights*. The large white house on its right is the *Paul Dudley Woodbridge Tavern*, now the residence of Hon. F.O. Emerson. A little beyond and across the road is *Coventry Hall*, owned by Rev. Frank Sewall of Washington. Here President Madison was entertained.

Leaving the village, we pass the *soldier's monument*, cross the railroad again at Norton's turnout, where we may see to the right *Lake Gorges* and the river and then descend under the brow of *Sentry Hill* to York Harbor Post Office. The Harbor is the mecca of wealthy people from all over the country and we pass many fine residences as the car climbs the hill that overlooks the harbor mouth and the bathing beach known as *Short Sands*. The tract sloping east from the summit of the hill is called *Norwood Farm* and from here is a fine view of *Long Beach*, the *Nubble* with its lighthouse and the wooded hills with, *Mount Agamenticus* rising in the distance. We pass along *Long Beach* siding and then follow the curving strand. Near the ruined cellar on the left, the first summer resident Hon. Henry C. Lord of Cincinnati erected a cottage in 1865. The island far out to sea is *Boone Island* and is the haunt of fishing and sailing parties. The next siding is *Sea Cottage* and soon after leaving it, the track swerves inland and emerges at the Western end of *York Beach*. On the bluff at the right is *Concordville*, while the hotels in the distance are on *Union Bluff*. Our car stops at the square within a minute's walk of the beach. Here we may spend the day, or, if we are so inclined, take a car for points further east over the recently completed short line to Kennebunk.

Tourists posing in an abandoned trolley car. Courtesy of Helen Vincent.

Workmen remove the tracks in front of the old bank building in York Village.

The last trolley passing through Badger's Island on March 17, 1923.

Epilog

November 12, 1897

The Electrics

The electrics are here, they have come to stay. We never fought their coming into town. We did think they took the wrong route, we think so still. But as they are here and came as they pleased, the only thing to do is make the best of it. We find them very convenient, especially since the steam road gives us only two trains a day; one in the morning before we "rich people" are supposed to be up, and the other arriving in the evening; each giving to the businessman too many hours in Portsmouth.

We must give the conductors and motormen on the electric road the credit of being the most gentlemanly, courteous and accommodating of men. We ride frequently on the road and have the opportunity to observe that they are real gentlemen, and surely the public appreciates such conduct in officials.

The management has recently added a steamer which runs each hour from Kittery Point to Newcastle and return. There are many people in York who have friends at Newcastle and vice versa. People living in Portsmouth have the same privilege, something they never had before, although living very near.

The electric people, under the management of Superintendent Meloon, are trying to win success by deserving it, which is a very strong way to win.

THE ELECTRIC CAR is one means of transportation which came into being quickly, mushroomed into prosperity, and faded rapidly. It was made possible by cheap electric power at the turn of the century. In Maine, as in the rest of New England, the former horse-car lines had expanded tremendously at the turn of the century.

At one time, it was possible to ride almost anywhere in Maine, New Hampshire, Massachusetts, Rhode Island and Connecticut — even to New York and points beyond—by street car. The lines flourished until after World War I, then began to decline. Most of the rails were pulled and sold for scrap in World War II. Other lines failed when buses took their place.

The street car reached the height of its glory in Maine about 1925. Many a Maine citizen has never seen a street car, much less ridden on a summer day in one of those open cars through which the wind rushed delightfully, removing the cares of the world. Since 1945 - 1946 the Public Utilities Commission's biennial reports have not even mentioned electric car lines.

On December 31, 1925, the heyday of these lines in Maine, their total assets were $73,793,000, including $60,773,000 in property investments. Profits totaled $1,893,000 for that year, but five of the fifteen companies reporting showed losses. In that same year, 1925, these electric railways carried almost twenty million passengers in Maine.

The successor to these lines was the automobile, which, operating over better highways, quickly brought about another major transformation in travel methods.[4]

---

[4] Herbert, Richard A., *Modern Maine It's Historic Background, People and Resources Vol. I.*, New York, Lewis Historical Publishing Co., 1951, pp. 601–602

Index

accidents, 43, 45, 68
Adams, J.Q., 47
Agamenticus, 75, 76
Alfred (ME), 37, 38, 39
Alfred jail, 29
Alice Howard (ferryboat), 3
America (naval vessel), 72
ancient burying ground, 76
Arbor Day, 52
Atlantic House, 35
Atlantic Shore Railway, 71
Augusta (ME), 1, 2, 17, 24, 38, 41
Austin, G. Frank, 28, 29, 45
auto repair shop, 14 (illus.)
autographic registers, 8

Badger, Capt. William, 72
Badger's Island, 2, 3, 4, 11, 21, 45, 52, 53 (illus.), 54 (illus.), 55, 61, 67, 68, 72, 76 (illus.), 78 (illus.)
Badger's Island trestle, 70 (illus.)
Baker, Orvill D., 1
Bald Head, 66
Bald Head Cliff Station, 44 (illus.)
Ball & Wood engines, 7
bank building, 79 (illus.)
Bartlett House, 17
Bath (ME), 67
bear, 4
Biddeford Journal, 12
Biddeford Times, 45
bill in equity, 29
blacksmith shop, 14 (illus.)

Blake, Mr. & Mrs. Samuel, 63
Bone & Young, 14 (illus.)
Boon Island, 76
Boston, 13, 21, 24, 33, 41, 51, 52
Boston & Maine Railroad, 2, 13, 31, 40, 41
Bowden, Charles, 67
Brave Boat Harbor, 16 (illus.), 21, 22, 75
Brave Boat Harbor trestle, 5 (illus.), 73 (illus.)
Bray House, 74
Bray, Majorie, 74
Breakers Hotel, 62 (illus.)
Bridge Hill, 73
Bridgeton (ME), 67
Briggs Carriage Company, 3, 16 (illus.)
Briggs open car, 42 (illus.)
Brixham (ME), 56
Browning, Robert, 73
Brownstone (ferryboat), 3
Brunswick (ME), 69
Bullfinch, 75
Bunker Hill, 73

cafe, 4
Cape Neddick River, 3
Cape Neddick Village (ME), 66
capital stock, 20
car barn, 69, 74
Car No. 4, xii (illus.)
car shed, 65
car-following system, 8, 9

carhouse, 2, 13, 29, 41, 45
Ceres Street, 71
Champernowne, Capt. Francis, 73
Champernowne Hotel, 56
Champernowne siding, 73
charter, 1, 2, 8, 12, 23, 28, 37, 46 (illus.), 47, 52, 53 (illus.), 62, 67
Chauncey's Creek (ME), 40, 41, 74
Church Street, 4 (illus.)
Cincinnati, 76
civil engineer, 1
Clarkson, T. & Son, 66
Comers, contractor, 69
commissioners, county, 15, 24
commissioners, railroad, 4, 40, 41, 68
Concordville, 76
Coney Island, 31, 33
Conference building, 72
Congress Street, 68
Cottle's Hill, 72
County Courthouse, 76
Courant, 10 (illus.), 24, 25, 31
Coventry Hall, 76
Cutts House, 73
Cutts Island, 40, 41, 74
cyclometer, 11

dance hall 4, 58 (illus.)
Davidson, J.T., 24, 39, 40
Davis, Charley
  "Alphabetical," ii (illus.)
Declaration of Independence, 72

Deerings ice pond, 62
Dennett, Capt. William, 72
depot, 47
Donnell, Capt. Leander, 37
Donnell House, 37
double truck flatcar, 65 (illus.)
Dover (NH), 61, 72, 75

Earl, Raymond, 14 (illus.)
East Rochester (NH), 61
Eliot (ME), 72, 75
Ellis, F.A. & Co., 35
Emerson, F.O., 76
Emerson Hotel, 30 (illus.)
Emery, John W., 24
Emery Place, 63
Emery, Samuel W., 17
equity suit, 1
Erie City engine, 7
Evans, Henry E., 3, 12, 15

Fairfield (ME), 1, 12, 17, 24, 67
Fairmont Hotel, 63
fares, 8, 12, 63
ferry, 1, 3, 5, 11, 12, 37, 41, 49, 52, 53 (illus.), 55, 59, 71, 72
ferry landing, 2, 54 (illus.)
ferry station, 67
First Parish Church, 75
Fish, William, 24
Fort Head, 75
Fort Hill, 73
Fort McClary, 73
"Frankenstein Trestles," 57
freighthouse, 47
Frenchmen, 67
Frost, Walter, 6 (illus.)

Gaines, Clarence, 43
General Electric generators, 7
Gerald, Amos F., 1, 12, 17, 24, 29, 39, 40, 43, 49, 57, 61, 67
Gerrish Island, 26, 74
Gilman Moulton Park, 28 (illus.), 34 (illus.)
Globe, 38, 39
Goldenrod, 60 (illus.)
golf, 57, 75
Goodenough, H.B., 67
Gorgeana, 75
Gorges, Sir Ferdinando, 73, 74, 75
Gosnold, Bartholomew, 75

Government boat, 59
Government Street, 72
Grant, W.H., 43

Hardman, F.H., 11
Harraden, Fred, 47
Harris Cove, 11
Harvard, 72
Hawkes, Wilson L., 1
Hayes, Calvin, 1
Hazen's siding, 75
Heath, Herbert, 24, 25, 40, 55
high school, 64, 75
Hillcroft Inn, 36 (illus.)
Hogan, James, 61, 62
Howells, William Dean, 73
Hutchins Corner, 74

Iduna Spring Hotel, 45, 47, 50 (illus.), 51, 56
Iduna Spring Hotel Co., 37
Iduna Spring Water, 37
illumination, 57, 69
incorporators, 1
injunction, 1, 2, 38, 39, 45
insulators, 7
Isles of Shoals, 75
Italians, 29, 38, 39, 41

J.T. Lewis Road, 20
Jennison, Samuel E., 1
Jewell, Archie, 6 (illus.)
Junkins, S.W., 55, 56
Junkins Store, 14 (illus.)

Keen, Warren, 47
Kearsarge (naval vessel), 72
Kennebunk, 76
Kennebunk Beach, 47
Kennebunk River, 47
Kennebunkport, 47
Kittery (ferryboat), 3, 53 (illus.), 71, 72
Kittery (ME), 1, 4, 5, 5 (illus.), 11, 13, 15, 20, 21, 22, 24, 26, 29, 45, 49, 54 (illus.), 55, 64, 67, 69, 72, 75
Kittery Foreside (ME), 20, 66, 72, 74
Kittery Point (ME), xii (illus.), 1, 3, 7, 11, 17, 20, 21, 22, 23, 26, 28, 29, 38, 40, 45, 46 (illus.), 47, 52, 53 (illus.), 55, 59, 61, 66, 68, 72, 78
Kittery Point Bridge, 73
Kittery Point Church, 73

Laconia 13' open bench car, 70 (illus.)
Lady Pepperell House, 73
LaFayette Inn, 62 (illus.)
Lake Gorges, 76
Lancaster Building, 30 (illus.)
Lawrence, E.J., 24, 67
Libby, Isaac C., 1, 12, 17, 24, 43, 56, 59, 61, 67
library, 14 (illus.)
Littlefield, Lyman, 14 (illus.)
Lock's Cove, 72
locomotive, 65 (illus.)
Long Beach, 20, 22, 49, 50 (illus.), 51, 63, 76
Long Sands Road, 4
Lord, Henry C., 76
Lowell, 17

Madison, President, 75
mail, 3, 8, 9
mail car, ii, 3
Mail Car A, ii (illus.)
Mail Car 108, 91 (illus.)
mail-closed pouch, 9
Main Street, 24, 25
Maine Legislature, 12, 13, 61
Macomber, George E., 2
Manchester (NH) 56, 69
Marden, Capt. Henry A., 41, 52
Marshall, Edward S., 37
Marshall, Fred W., 52, 56
Marshall, George A., 37
Marshall House Hotel, 37
Massachusetts Plantation, 72
Mason, John, 73
Masons, 66
McClary, Major, 73
McClure, Charles F., 1
McIntire, David, 61
McIntire, Melvin, 56
Meloon, supt., 64
menagerie, 4, 58 (illus.)
Mercer, Mrs., 57
Mercer's Corner, 28 (illus.)
Milliken, Charles, 17
Mitchell, Horace, 1, 11, 17, 24, 39, 40
Moody, Edward C., 37
Moses, Gilman C., 67
Moulton, Allen C., 38
Moulton, Frank A., 68
Moulton, Hayes, 29
Mystic (ferryboat), 3

Naval Prison, 72
Navy Yard, 12, 72
Nevers Carriage Company, 14 (illus.)
New Hampshire Legislature, 61
New March (ferryboat), 3, 67
Newmarch, Capt. John, 72
Newmarch Street, 72
New York (NY), 33, 51
Newburyport Herald, 71
Newcastle (NH), 59, 69
North Ware, 56
Norton's Trestle, 42 (illus.), 76
Norwood Farm Road, 2
Norwood Farms, 36 (illus.), 76
Norwood, John E., 1
Nubble, 61, 76
Nye, S.A., 67
Nye, S.H., 24

Ocean House, 35
Ogunquit Village, 66
Old Gaol, 76
Old Home Week, 75
Organug, 75
Organug Road, 75

Paper Mill, 72
Parade, 71
Paris (FR), 51
Parsonage, 73, 76
Passaconaway, Inn, 37
passengers, 44 (illus.)
Pepperell Mansion House, 74
Pepperell, William (Elder), 73, 74
Pepperell, Sir William, 73
Pickering House, 28 (illus.), 34 (illus.)
picnic grounds, 58 (illus.)
pile, 5, 59
pile driver, 40, 49
piling, 20, 38, 40
Pine Tree State, 71
Piscataqua, 72
Piscataqua River, 1, 12, 71
Piscataqua Yacht Club, 73
Plaisted, George F., 10 (illus.), 11, 15
Plaisted's Store, 14 (illus.)
poles, 7, 21
Portsmouth (NH), 1, 3, 5, 8, 11, 12, 13, 15, 17, 21, 24, 25, 38, 47, 49, 51, 54 (illus.), 56, 57, 59, 63, 67, 68, 71

Portsmouth Bridge, 2, 11, 72
Portsmouth Bridge Co., 37
Portsmouth Times, 52
Portsmouth River, 37
Portland (ME), 21, 38
post office car, 3
Post Road, 20, 21, 22, 25
power station (power house), 2, 29, 40, 52, 53 (illus.), 55, 62, 74
Prince, Clarence, M., 1
Public Utilities Commission, 80

rails, 7, 17, 28, 29, 30 (illus.), 35, 41, 45
Raleigh (naval vessel), 72
Rayne's Neck, 21, 75
restaurant, 58 (illus.)
Rice Memorial Library, 72
Rice's Bridge, 20, 21, 24
Rochester (NH), 58 (illus.)
Rollins, Governor, 75
rotary substation, 75
Rowell, Frank E., 1
Russo-Japanese War, 72

Saco, 43
St. Andrews Lodge, 66
St. Aspinquid Park, 3, 58 (illus.)
St. John's Church, 3, 71
St. Louis Car Co., 3
St. Louis closed car, cover (illus.), 44
Sands Motel, 62 (illus.)
Santiago, battle of, 72
Sawyer, Capt. Charles, 55
Scotland, 56, 61
Scruton, Leon E., 1
Sea Cottage, 76
Sea Point, 56, 68, 74
Seabrook (NH), 43
Seabury, 3, 21, 22, 42 (illus.), 47, 75
Seabury Station, 21, 63, 75
Seavey's Island, 72
Sewall, Rev. Frank, 76
Sewall, Major Samuel, 75
Sentry Hill, 75
Sewall's Bridge, 3, 21, 48 (illus.), 57, 63, 75
Short Sands, 76
sign shop, 14 (illus.)
sleepers, 20
Smith, Capt. John, 71
snowplow, 3
Soldier's Monument, 76

South Berwick (ME), 15, 75
Southerly (prison ship), 72
Spanish prisoners, 72
Sparhawk House, 73
Spinney, W.T., 66
Spruce Creek, 21, 22, 73
stage coaches, 50 (illus.)
Staples, John E., 37
Staples, Lewis E., 17
State Supreme Court, 2, 15, 39
steamer, 3, 55, 56, 71
Stevens, Daniel A., 37, 66
Stover, John, 68
Strawbery Banke, 71
street sprinkler, 62
Suncook Valley, 56
Swett, Jethro H., 1

Talpey, E.A., 38, 66, 67, 68
Thaxter, Levi, 73
Thaxter's Station, 63
tickets, school, 8
tickets, reduced rate, 8
ties, 7, 26, 29, 30 (illus.)
Town Hall, 76
Town Meeting, 21, 22, 24, 26, 27
Town Records, 38, 39
Trafton, Charles Oscar, 45
Traip Academy, 72
Treaty of Portsmouth, 72
trestles, 2, 5, 5 (illus.), 16 (illus.), 42 (illus.)
trestles, "Frankenstein," 57
Twitchell, F.H., 67

Union Bluff, 11, 76

Varrell House, 34 (illus.)
Varrell House Annex, 34 (illus.)
Vermule, Abraham, 37
Village Green (York), 75

waiting rooms, 2, 8, 35, 54 (illus.), 69, 75 (illus.)
Walker, Wilson M., 40, 66
Washington (DC), 40, 45
Washington, George, 71
Wason, 3
Wason 20' box car, 73 (illus.)
Wasson, George, 74
Waterville (ME), 1, 4, 12, 17, 24, 67
Waterville Trust Co., 4
Wentworth-by-the-Sea, 17
Wentworths, 71

main

385 B247 Me.Coll.   c.2
Bardwell, John D.
A diary of the Portsmouth,
 Kittery, and York electric

PORTLAND PUBLIC LIBRARY
5 MONUMENT SQUARE
PORTLAND, MAINE 04101

	DATE DUE	
JAN 0 3 1994		
FEB 2 2 1996		
NOV 1 5 1996		
OCT 0 5 2000		
DEC 2 6 2008		